REMOTE, NOT DISTANT

PRAISE FOR
REMOTE, NOT DISTANT

"*Remote, Not Distant* will help you stay ahead of the curve in the remote revolution. Everyone – not just leaders – will benefit from this comprehensive and actionable collection of insights, ideas, and tools to build a strong hybrid work culture. If you want to thrive in a post-pandemic world, read this book!"
   —Dr. Tasha Eurich, New York Times Bestselling Author of Insight and Bankable Leadership

"The future of work isn't fixed; it's waiting to be built. *Remote, Not Distant* offers a tactical blueprint to building a better future for all."
   —Darren Murph, Head of Remote, GitLab

"Gustavo Razzetti captures the return to the office/remote debate so well and enables us to understand how we can utilize the benefits of remote working and not compromise on having a great company culture. He offers practical tips on how to overcome the obstacles of remote/hybrid work. A great read!"
   —Liz Rider, Global Head of Leadership and Culture, Volvo

"*Remote Not Distant* provides ample evidence and examples of how to build the culture you want and the types of collaboration you need, using flexible solutions that work for your team."
   —Brian Elliott, Senior Vice President, Slack

"It is not too overblown to say this is a book that every leader of remote teams needs to have by their side. A highly practical, no-nonsense, 'how-to' guide to restore and improve workplace culture in a complex world."
　—Anish Hindocha, Change Lead, ITV

"Tremendously insightful guide with immediate practical application (chapter-ending recaps, tools, and tips). Grounded in the latest learnings from a broad array of industry practitioners, academics, and consulting thought leaders. This book will help leaders address a mission-critical blind spot in their current thinking about the post-pandemic world and the ramifications and implications of not meeting work colleagues 'where they live.'"
　—Andrew O'Hearn, Associate Director,
　　Change Management, Bayer

"The pandemic has shaken workplace culture's old paradigms, yet this is so recent that most leaders lack the knowledge as to how to navigate it. Gustavo Razzetti has broken down the puzzle and provides frameworks and actionable tools, allowing you to create your own blueprint for success. *Remote, Not Distant* is a critical read for anyone interested in gaining thoughtful perspectives and actionable paths as to how to navigate the new normal."
　—Silvina Cendra, Head of Customer Marketing Strategy, Taco Bell

"At a time when we need to rethink leadership, *Remote, Not Distant* is an important book that delivers a roadmap to anyone who wants to be successful in our new world! Bravo!"
　—Hortense le Gentil—Executive Leadership Coach and author
　　of Aligned.

"*Remote, Not Distant* is a treasure box of insights and tools to build new hybrid work solutions. Gustavo Razzetti concretely guides us to take the best from our experiences without proposing salvific

recipes. A great support in looking at the future and starting to build it."
—Letizia Migliola, Business Consultant, Italy

"Gustavo Razzetti has created a resource that demystifies hybrid work and facilitates its adoption in a practical way. Starting with basic human needs such as belonging and safety, Gustavo sets the tone of what it means to create a sustainable culture. This book is a must-read for everyone who is ready and eager to dive beyond the surface of hybrid and go the extra mile."
—Dr. Myriam Hadnes, Founder, Never Done Before

"*Remote, Not Distant* offers practical and tactical stories, solutions, and scenarios that are proven to work. Gustavo has compiled a great resource to help you on your journey as we all navigate this transformative time in the workforce. These are not theories but an extension to his existing body of work around culture design and collaboration."
—Douglas Flory, Global Practice Lead, GoTo

"I learned so much from this book – relatable stories, practical tips, and evidence-based research contribute to a very valuable, thoughtful, well-paced, and intelligent book that is accessible, not too long, and provided me with new ways of considering hybrid and online engagement situations."
—Susan Raphael, Principal Consultant, Australia

"One of the reasons some companies are clamoring for a return to the offices is that they have not yet found the viable replacement for that sense of connectedness. Gustavo's book is a timely blueprint for restoring and enhancing team cultures in the new age of permanent hybrid work. Well sourced and thought through, methodically organized, and clearly articulated, it's a step-by-step guide to help you identify and fill the gaps created by physical

distance and turn your teams once again into the well-adjusted, humming, and happy engines of productivity."
—Katya Sylvester, Senior Manager, Change Management, Fannie Mae

"Culture. Belonging. Purpose. Engagement. Rituals. Ideas like these are difficult to define, let alone get right in an organization. By challenging long-held assumptions and sharing surprising examples, extensive research, and highly actionable tools, Razzetti shows us that it's not magic after all. Anyone who is truly committed to helping hybrid or remote workplaces thrive, despite continued uncertainty and ambiguity, will find the book an invaluable, transformative companion on the journey."
—Maren Gube, Ph.D., Executive Director, Resiliti

REMOTE, NOT DISTANT

Design a **Company Culture** That Will
Help You Thrive in a **Hybrid Workplace**

GUSTAVO RAZZETTI

LIBERATIONIST
PRESS

Liberationist Press
597 Hyacinth Pl
Highland Park, IL 60035
USA

ISBNs
Hardback 978-0-9990973-8-0
Paperback 978-0-9990973-9-7
Ebook78-0-9990973-6-6
Kindle ASIN: B09VXX4FN3

Library of Congress Control Number: 2022909745

Editing: Sarah Barbour
Cover design: Krishna Mohan
Interior design and typesetting: Adina Cucicov

TABLE OF CONTENTS

Introduction

YOU DON'T NEED AN OFFICE TO BUILD CULTURE

Welcome to the beginning of the end of the workplace as we know it. Normal is gone. The culture that got you here won't get you there.

When Apple CEO Tim Cook announced the return to the office, he didn't anticipate the backlash.

The new policy stated that everyone should work from Apple Park on Mondays, Tuesdays, and Wednesdays. Cook emphasized that the move would reenergize Apple's culture, which relies on strong in-person relationships.

Or so he thought.

In fact, most people weren't so happy about returning to the office. A letter[1] written and edited by 80 employees reminded Cook of how they delivered:

> the same quality of products and services that Apple is known for, all while working almost completely remotely."

> Over the last year, we often felt not just unheard, but at times, actively ignored. Messages like, "we know many of you are eager to reconnect in person with your colleagues back in the office" with no messaging acknowledging that there are directly contradictory feelings among us feels dismissive and invalidating.

Even worse, employees thought that the new policy forced them to choose "between either a combination of our families, our well-being, and being empowered to do our best work, or being a part of Apple."

Cook was taken aback. Not only were the employees challenging the three-days-a-week approach, they were questioning the value of being in the office *at all*.

Apple was not the only company that failed to understand the new reality of work. Citibank, Google, and American Airlines, just to name a few, also missed how the pandemic transformed our relationship with work. They expected people to go back to normal as if nothing happened.

As Oracle content manager Lauren Pope wrote: "I find it interesting (stupid) how WFH [working from home] was considered a 'vital necessity' to keep companies afloat last year... But now that companies want employees back in the office—fully remote work is being treated like a recruiting perk. How are you going to tell employees they need to "prove" they've earned the "privilege" of remote work?"[2]

The problem is that most organizations were forced to switch to a work-from-home model and failed to change their way of thinking. CEOs still believe that company culture is only achieved when people are together.

But it doesn't have to be that way. You can work remotely and still be connected. You don't need an office to feel like you're part of a team.

As I'm writing this, most companies have once again postponed (some indefinitely) returning to the office. This provides a unique opportunity to reset your culture and leverage the best of both worlds: in-person and remote.

Now more than ever, a strong culture is crucial for driving positive results. *Remote, Not Distant* will help you build an anywhere/anytime culture to adapt and succeed in a hybrid workplace.

Before we get started, though, let me tell you why I wrote this book.

As CEO of Fearless Culture, a workplace culture consulting firm, I help teams become the best version of themselves. Although I've facilitated several remote workshops throughout the years, the majority of my work has been in person. Maybe because I spent much of my career in office-centric organizations, I always thought that strong collaboration required being in the same place at the same time.

And then the pandemic hit. I was just about to start a global roadshow to facilitate my Culture Design Masterclass in Toronto, New York, London, Barcelona, Amsterdam, Sydney, and many other cities. I had to cancel my plans and convert my consulting and workshops to virtual formats.

Long story short, I had to consider how to design and facilitate sessions. I couldn't simply replicate the in-person experience in the remote world; I had to think differently.

In addition to helping thousands of people design better workplace cultures, I had to help them learn how to work remotely—from facilitating virtual meetings and using MURAL to giving feedback remotely and collaborating asynchronously.

I've spent countless hours researching and creating tools for remote collaboration, talking to leaders and employees, and listening and learning from workshop participants. Eventually, I decided to write a book to share what I've learned with the global community but I didn't limit this to personal experience; I interviewed hundreds of generous experts around the world—from fully remote organizations and best-selling authors to Fortune 500 senior leaders and consultants.

 The most important thing to remember is that this is a journey. You'll save a lot of time by beginning with the strong foundation this book provides. It is not a silver bullet but a roadmap to jump-start your own discovery.

One note before we dive in: People often use the terms "hybrid," "remote-first," and "remote" interchangeably. However, there are important differences that have vital implications in terms of operations, flexibility, and norms.

Let's start with the two extremes: co-located and fully remote (or all-remote). In a co-located situation, everyone works the same place on same schedule—it's office-centric. In contrast, an all-remote company has no office. Team members and leaders alike work wherever and whenever they choose.

A hybrid arrangement includes people who work fully at the office, entirely from home, or both. At one end of the spectrum, the hybrid is office-centric. Employees are still expected to spend a good amount of time physically in the office, and the company doesn't really change how it operates. On the other end of the spectrum, the company radically evolves its culture and practices to create an equal experience for all workers whether remote or in-office.

(We'll do a deeper dive into this spectrum in Step 5: Release Agility.)

For the purpose of this book, I will use the term "hybrid" or "distributed" to refer to the whole hybrid spectrum. And I will use "remote-first," "digital-first," or "virtual-first" for organizations that have intentionally created a culture and workflow focused on serving the distributed workforce.

In the following pages, we'll explore the challenges of a hybrid workplace. We'll review top-performing remote cultures and what makes them tick. We'll also discover actionable insights, ideas, tools, and activities that you can implement immediately.

This book enables you to increase connectedness and collaboration in a distributed workforce using a five-step roadmap.

Foundation provides an explanation of workplace culture: what it is, what it isn't, why it's important, and how you can begin to examine your own. This lays the groundwork for the rest of the book.

Step 1 is to reset your culture. We'll address the five mindset shifts required to succeed in a hybrid workplace and how you can build a strong remote culture, regardless of where your team members work from.

Step 2 challenges the idea of alignment. Rather than having a vision imposed on them, team members want to be part of the process. We'll review how to reimagine a shared future with a team purpose to define clear priorities and expected behaviors.

Step 3 focuses on belonging; ensuring that team members feel safe enough to bring their full selves to work, challenge the status quo, and come up with innovative ideas. We'll address how to build a culture of inclusion, connection, and feedback.

Step 4 is a deep dive into the six modes of collaboration in a hybrid workplace. We'll review the different types, which to use when, and why teams must default to asynchronous communication.

Step 5 covers how to increase speed, adaptability, and decision-making. We'll examine how your team makes decisions, revisit norms and rules, and explore how to release agility.

If you're thirsty for more, you'll find exercises throughout the book to help your team design a hybrid culture that works.

Each step includes a "Your Turn" activity with a QR code to download the respective tool. You'll be able to download additional valuable resources at the end of the book, plus find a *surprise* to help you on your journey.

Designing a remote culture is a never-ending job. Get ready to experiment with new concepts and tools. Most importantly, let go of "the way we do things here" and make room for new ideas.

Empty your cup and enjoy the journey.

FOUNDATION

FOUNDATION

WHAT IS CULTURE? (AND WHY DOES IT MATTER, ANYWAY?)

The pandemic has put "the way we do things around here" to the test, and culture matters now more than ever. But before we talk about how to upgrade your workplace culture and thrive in a hybrid workplace, let's discuss the concept of culture and why you should care.

These days, allusions to workplace culture clutter up our social media feeds with memes and clever sayings. Job postings boast of "fun," "casual," or "work hard, play hard" company cultures. Many people think culture is about perks such as ping-pong tables, free beer, and fancy food.

Free yoga lessons and sushi are nice. However, culture is much more than that; it's the environment that helps people do their best work.

Maybe a good place to start is by first looking at what culture is *not*.

Culture eats strategy for breakfast.

This saying, which pops up regularly in LinkedIn feeds, is often attributed to Peter Drucker, but there's no evidence he said it.

It's a vastly oversimplified approach to what culture is and, more importantly, it creates an unnecessary conflict. While I'm not the first to extol the importance of culture, it's a mistake to pit culture against strategy, as if one is more important than the other.

Culture and strategy are not rivals; they're two sides of the same coin. A strong culture amplifies a strong strategy, but it won't do you any good without the *right* strategy. You need both.

Intentionally designed cultures not only increase employee engagement but also produce stronger business results. Both science and common sense tell you that a positive workplace culture creates a positive business impact. Research shows that organizations with healthy workplace cultures outperform weak or toxic ones.[3] A study by Glassdoor shows that companies with a strong culture beat even the Standard & Poor's 500 Index, delivering almost twice the gain.[4]

Culture is an iceberg. Some is visible at first sight, but much of it is below the waterline and out of sight.

This is another misleading cliché, and wrongly attributed to Edgar Schein, an MIT professor known for his ground-breaking work on the organizational culture model. Schein dislikes this metaphor. He believes that "unlike an iceberg, culture is not in a frozen, solid state."

On a good day, culture feels invisible. On a bad day, it's too obvious. No one notices a smooth performance, but toxic behaviors quickly catch the eye.

The idea that culture is invisible reinforces the feeling that it's abstract and difficult to act upon. Culture design, however, uses tools and conversations to make people more aware of beliefs and behaviors that shape the culture around them. This awareness enables them to positively and pro-actively become more intentional about molding culture.

The way we do things around here.

I like this definition a bit better because it addresses behavior, which at least is measurable. The cultural system, however, goes beyond behavior (i.e., what people do and how they do it). It also includes how people feel (emotions) and how they think (mindsets). These three elements together act as a system.

What Culture Does

While people still tend to think in terms of what culture looks like (casual Fridays, nap pods, and so forth), it's more helpful to think in terms of what culture *accomplishes*. A strong culture produces the following five effects:

Culture supports results

Anything that is measured and watched improves.
—Bob Parsons, GoDaddy founder

Most people still think of culture as "soft" or "fluffy," however, its impact is anything but weak.

Research by Professor James L. Heskett shows that a strong culture can increase performance by 20–30% compared to "culturally unremarkable" competitors.[5] According to the Organizational Health Index, companies with the strongest culture can perform *200% higher* than those in the bottom quartile.[6]

Culture creates teams

You need the right people with you, not the best people.
—Jack Ma, Alibaba cofounder

One of the most critical roles of workplace culture is the process of sense-making.[7] It creates a shared identity that generates both attraction and rejection.

Culture is the glue that brings people together, protecting the system from "wrong people" and "wrong behaviors."

Culture gives employees meaning

Make sure everybody in the company has great opportunities, has a meaningful impact, and is contributing to the good of society.
—Larry Page, Google cofounder

Culture is a carrier of meaning. It provides not only a shared view of "what is," but also of "why." Your organizational culture turns work into something meaningful, not just a job.

Culture is your North Star; it inspires and guides your people to achieve something bigger than themselves.

Healthy cultures adapt better to change

A company's culture is the foundation for future innovation. An entrepreneur's job is to build the foundation.
—Airbnb CEO Brian Chesky

Organizations with high-performing cultures thrive on change. The opposite also holds true: unhealthy cultures do not respond well to change.

Research by McKinsey shows that 70% of organizational transformations fail because of culture-related issues.[8]

Culture boosts (or destroys) employee motivation

Employee Engagement arises out of culture and not the other way around.
—Moe Carrick and Cammie Dunaway, authors of
  Fit Matters: How to Love Your Job

Company culture is vital because it makes work more pleasant. When people's values and purpose align with those of an organization, they are more likely to enjoy working there. According to a study by Deloitte, 95% of employees say that culture is more important than compensation.[9]

Clearly, a healthy culture makes a difference. Moreover, as we'll discuss throughout this book, culture can be deliberately shaped to serve your company, much as a fruit tree is pruned to keep it healthy and productive.

Your Culture Is a System

Leaders often think that having a set of core values or a purpose statement is the same as defining their company culture. However, culture is more than that. It's a complex, interconnected system. Great leaders focus both on the forest *and* the trees.

Schein likes to say that *culture is dynamic, not static.* It's constantly evolving, yet stable and strong. It can be shaped but not changed. Schein uses the lily pond as a metaphor for culture; it's a living ecosystem that's constantly changing.

Everything is interconnected. The things you see above the surface are nurtured from below.

After decades of experience in the marketing and innovation world working with Fortune 500 companies, start-ups, and everything in between, I've realized that most organizations don't lack ideas, talent, or resources. What they lack is a conducive culture. They need a better system to liberate their true potential.

It's my mission to make culture conversations more tangible, to discover a method of purposefully building culture as a system. As a result, I developed the Culture Design Canvas, a visual framework that helps codify the three areas of culture:

- The Core
- Emotional Culture
- Functional Culture

The **Core** is the foundation of culture, defining a shared future that everyone aspires to. It includes purpose and values, priorities, and outlines which behaviors are rewarded and which are punished.

Emotional Culture helps create belonging. It encompasses psychological safety, feedback, and rituals.

Functional Culture defines your company's agility. It includes decision-making, meetings, norms, and rules.

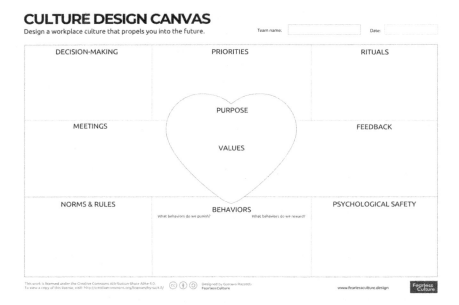

Use this QR code to download your own free copy of the Culture Design Canvas.

Every company has a culture by chance or by choice, but successful cultures are the result of intentional design.

To borrow a phrase from social planners Horst Rittel and Melvin Webber, culture is a "wicked problem," meaning that it can't be solved, it can only be worked on. There are no quick fixes, no simple, straightforward solutions. Thriving in a hybrid workplace requires experimentation, iteration, and an ongoing commitment.

The following principles describe my approach to culture design.

Human-centric

Culture Design is about building a culture based on people's needs and using feedback to continually improve it. The approach starts with the employee in mind and how they perceive their organization's culture and what is or isn't working.

Systemic

Every organization has a system that shapes the behavior of its employees. Increasing performance and innovation requires focusing on the forest rather than the trees.

Co-created

Leaders play a critical role in defining their company culture and modeling expected behaviors. However, it's people's behavior that actually shapes the culture. Culture design is a co-creative process. Smart leaders tap into the collective wisdom to find solutions that will help improve theirs.

Experimental and iterative

Culture design is an iterative process, not a one-time activity. What worked yesterday most probably won't work tomorrow, so be prepared to adapt. This is even more critical in a hybrid environment.

Evolving

Remember, culture design is a journey, not a destination. It's a never-ending job. Think in terms of building on what's working while improving or eliminating what's not.

So, how can you apply these principles to build culture remotely?

You need to reset and evolve your culture. You must design what I call an "Anywhere/Anytime Culture" that connects people and helps them do their best work, regardless of when and from where they work.

The rest of this book will guide you through the Anywhere/Anytime Culture roadmap necessary to create and maintain a healthy, vibrant culture in a hybrid workplace.

An Anywhere/Anytime Culture
The 5 Steps

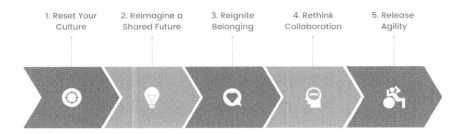

The roadmap has five steps:

1. **Reset Your Culture**
2. **Reimagine a Shared Future**
3. **Reignite Belonging**
4. **Rethink Collaboration**
5. **Release Agility**

In this book, we'll explore each of these steps in detail. Before we begin, one piece of advice. There are no shortcuts to thriving in a hybrid workplace. You must adopt a trial-and-error approach. Be ready to experiment, make mistakes, adjust your course, and iterate. Focus on making progress rather than on looking for the perfect solution.

Recap

FOUNDATION: WHAT IS CULTURE?

Culture is the environment that helps people do their best work.

Culture evolves naturally, but the most successful companies deliberately design theirs.

Culture is a "wicked problem." It cannot be "solved" once and for all; it must be continuously worked on.

Culture is an interconnected system of behavior, mindset, and emotions; it requires more than having a set of values.

RESET YOUR CULTURE

STEP 1

THE CULTURE THAT GOT YOU HERE WON'T GET YOU THERE

The hybrid workplace is here to stay.

Even before the pandemic, around a quarter of employed Americans were working from home at least some of the time, and more than half had flexible schedules. Despite that, there was still a stigma associated with remote work. However, COVID-19 quickly shifted work dynamics. Not only did it debunk most of the myths about working remotely, it actually increased productivity to unexpected levels.[10] And, as the incident at Apple shows, many employees appreciate the flexibility and freedom that remote work has given them.

A hybrid workplace can bring together the best of both worlds—the convenience of working from home and the social interactions of the office.

Unfortunately, many companies are slipping back into old, unhealthy habits rather than building on what they learned during the pandemic. In doing so, they're missing a golden opportunity to embrace the future.

Digging your heels in, going back to the office, and pretending the pandemic never happened is a mistake. And trying to take in-office cultures and practices and copy-paste them into a half-remote/half-in-office experience can backfire.

Hybrid could quickly become the worst of both worlds.

As Betsy Bula, a GitLab all-remote evangelist, told me: "Companies are struggling. They use hybrid as something they can lean on—a temporary Band-Aid in the meantime, to try to meet and please the needs of all team members that are very different for their work."

As a whole, hybrid is difficult to do right.

You need to be intentional about revisiting (almost) everything about your culture. It will require a lot of experimentation and adjustments to avoid creating a two-tier experience; one for remote, one for co-located employees.

After eight months of being forced to work fully from home due to the pandemic, GoTo, the company behind tools such as GoToMeeting, LastPass, and RescueAssist had three choices, Douglas Flory, global practice lead, shared with me. "We could renew ourselves, we could return, or we could refresh." Using a house as a metaphor for culture, he remembers telling the CEO, "We could paint it, we could go back to the house as is, or we could move to a new house."

Like most companies, GoTo had an office-centric culture that wasn't suitable for the new reality. In October 2020, CEO Mike Kohlsdorf officially declared, "We are becoming a remote-first company."

The decision to refresh instead of a return or a simple renewal was a pivotal moment for the company. GoTo is currently experiencing its strongest culture—and business growth—as a result of a hybrid workplace where people can choose when and where to work.

I invite you to seize this unique chance: Consciously design a successful hybrid workplace that bridges the gap between what employees want and what leaders demand.

It's time for a reset.

As companies reopen their offices, they face new challenges. Step 1: Reset is not about getting rid of everything and starting from scratch. It's about leveraging what's worked in the past *and* adopting new behaviors as needed. It's time to create an Anywhere/ Anytime Culture, one that brings the people in your organization together regardless of where they're working from.

THE 5 KEY MINDSET SHIFTS

To thrive in a hybrid workplace, your organization needs to adopt five key mindset shifts. Let's examine each one, as they form the basis for much of the culture design work we'll be doing.

From Culture by Chance to Culture by Design

Many people believe that culture just happens organically; that's why they're afraid it will suffer if people are not at the office. But culture can and, I would argue, *should* be designed deliberately. A successful company culture doesn't happen by accident. It is designed and built with purpose and intent.

It's true that, left to its own devices, company culture is organic; it will happen naturally and emerge freely. However, in a hybrid environment, you need to be more intentional. Company culture design should be treated just as intentionally as designing a new product. It should start and end with the user in mind, turning it into a co-creation process.

Very few companies have had the privilege of working remotely for years—and by choice, not forced by a global pandemic. One common thread I observed researching successful remote-first organizations is their obsession with designing culture intentionally, along with a healthy emphasis on clarity and transparency.

Web development company Automattic, best known for its WordPress product, considers communication "the oxygen of a distributed company." Its employees are encouraged to communicate as much as possible, not only about work, but also about personal things. From a formal approach to informal communication to codifying the obvious, a remote-first culture is the result of obsessive design and intention.

Another big lesson is to adopt a trial-and-error mindset. No one gets it right from day one. Companies like GitLab, Doist, and Google have been experimenting for over a decade, and their approach to remote work continues to evolve.

 Most importantly, involve your people. Successful remote-first organizations co-design their cultures with their employees.[11]

At GitLab, anyone can edit the company values. You're encouraged to make suggestions even if you don't work there. Give it a try: Contact GitLab's CEO Sid Sijbrandij on Twitter with any suggestions you have.[12]

Culture design isn't about imposing a path, but rather building a framework through continuous input from people and iteration.

Later in this book, I go into more detail about exactly how to design culture. For now, I'd simply like to impress upon you that intentionality, or lack of, can make or break your hybrid culture.

From Input to Impact

Historically, organizations have rewarded input—visibility, effort, presenteeism, etc.—over outcome. Employees who worked late, sent a lot of emails, or were always in meetings were perceived as hard-working, committed team players.

Organizations can benefit enormously by shifting their focus away from these traditional input measures and focusing on impact. Don't reward presenteeism or long hours. Evaluate people based on goals and results, not on how late they stay in the office or how many Zoom calls they attend.

Google has been using OKRs (objectives and key results) at both an organizational and team level since long before the pandemic. OKRs form a "binding contract" among team members, according to Google VP of Digital Work Experience Prasad Setty. OKRs help divide roles and responsibilities, encouraging people to think in terms of contribution, not input. "As long as the goals are clear and OKRs are clear, you don't need to monitor activity/input," Setty explained.[13]

It's important to focus on metrics beyond goals. In Europe, Microsoft encourages people to consider learning and growth in addition to OKRs. People must reflect on questions such as, What impact did I have personally? How did

I contribute to the success of others? How have I leveraged others' success to become better myself?

 Having a team purpose helps people focus on the most significant outcome—the impact you want to create in the world.

People want to be part of something bigger than themselves. They want to create a legacy. Having a purpose matters more than ever. Research by Humu shows that people who don't feel their work contributes to their company's purpose are six times more likely to quit their jobs than their peers who do.[14]

If you want engaged and productive employees, focus on the impact you want to create and they will follow.

From Work-Life Im/balance to Work-Life Integration

As a society, we tend to consider work and personal life separate, but for most of us, "work-life balance" remains elusive. Paradoxically, the more we try to pursue it, the harder it becomes to achieve.

"Always-on" culture was already breaking down the boundaries between our work and personal lives. Then the pandemic arrived, and the lines became blurrier than ever. Working from home has created a more human connection to work. Many of us have spent the majority of the last two years working in the company of pets, children, spouses, and roommates. COVID brought work to our homes, and our personal lives into our jobs.

At GitLab, team members hold "Juice Box" chats. These are similar to a coffee chat but aim to bring employees' children, grandchildren, and other family members together. These sessions are usually focused on a topic such as Legos, superheroes, video games, or outdoor activities. Instead of fighting reality and trying to prevent kids from interrupting business calls, GitLab went all-in, creating a kind of all-remote version of "Bring Your Child to Work Day" held multiple times a year.

Many companies have thrown away their perfectionist approach to the workplace with acts such as replacing professional dress codes with more informal ones. GoTo has revisited its core values through this lens. For example, "Be Real" now also means that's it's okay if your Internet connection freezes or your dog or child unexpectedly join a Zoom meeting. Being real means you are not expected to always look professional—overly polished or perfect—but human. This removes unnecessary pressure and helps people do a better job.

 Accepting the increasingly fluid boundaries between work and personal life, rather than building higher, stronger walls between them, will create a more humane and flexible workplace. Before, our daily commute created a clear boundary between personal life and work. Today, working just a few steps from where you sleep or play is common.

Microsoft CEO Satya Nadella says that harmony has been critical to his success and happiness. He doesn't really separate work and life, but instead frames it as work-life harmony. "I always used to think that you need to find that balance between what's considered relaxing and what's considered working."[15] Nadella encourages employees to follow his lead in trying to harmonize what you deeply care about with your work.

As Nadella stated: "If I'm happy at work, I am a better person at home, a better husband and a better father. And if I'm happy at home, I come into work more energized—a better employee and a better colleague."

From Synchronous to Asynchronous Collaboration

One of the biggest mistakes most companies made when forced to work remotely was carrying old habits into a new way of working. They continued approaching collaboration as something that needed to happen synchronously, with everyone reviewing information, making decisions, or brain-storming together.

The result? Most teams struggled with an overload of meetings, Zoom fatigue, and late hours, even on weekends.

Traditional workplaces were filled with synchronous communications. Meetings required everyone to show up, and people were expected to take calls and respond to emails immediately, regardless of what else was going on.

Amir Salihefendic, CEO of Doist, said the benefits of asynchronous communication go beyond flexibility "so people think before they write, and it creates a much more calm environment." At Doist, people can set their own work schedules, are not pressured to respond outside of work hours, and have the time and space to think about a topic and regroup with thoughtful responses.

Experts agree that whether your team is fully remote or hybrid, it should adopt an async-first approach.[16] Asynchronous collaboration creates a different, more flexible set of rules.

 Asynchronous communication requires more intentionality and effort. Your team needs to become obsessive about documentation which can slow down communication sometimes. However, when people are thinking deeply, writing down their ideas, and presenting them, better collaboration and work result—no meetings required.

Updates and information sharing don't require a meeting anymore. EMEA Partner Technical Lead for Microsoft Teams Rooms Michel Bouman suggests shifting from viewing meetings as a one-off experience to a life cycle. Before the meeting, coordinate schedules, share necessary information, and assign prework tasks. During the meeting, use the time for discussions and decision-making. After the meeting, each person takes care of their part and, if any discussion is required, it should happen asynchronously.

From One-Size-Fits-All to Flexibility

I get a lot of pushback when I tell my clients to set a simple, company-wide policy and then give teams the freedom to design their own hybrid approach. Organizations are used to having a one-size-fits-all approach to work. It can be hard for them to accept that the benefits of flexibility more than justify any complexities.

However, a common denominator of each successful remote company I interviewed for this book was that teams had a say in how things got done, from shaping the remote work corporate policy to having the flexibility to adapt them to their own needs.

Apple's mistakes included assuming that leadership understood what employees wanted and tried to find a solution that would work for everyone. Messages like "We know many of you are eager to reconnect in person with your colleagues back in the office" backfired. Employees often felt not just unheard but actively ignored, and Apple's assumptions made things worse. People felt that the mandate to go back to the office showed a lack of empathy.

Apple employees didn't just push back. They provided concrete, actionable solutions. Their complaint letter is a smart roadmap for redesigning the future of work.[17] Among other things, they suggested that

- Remote and location-flexible decisions be up to teams to decide (just like hiring decisions)
- A short survey be available to promote ongoing feedback on topics affecting hybrid work, including employee churn
- The company evaluate the environmental impact of going back to the office
- All employees could set their own schedules according to what would work best for them

 An overly rigid approach can create inequality in the workplace. Be intentional about creating an even experience for every employee, including equal access to leaders, career opportunities, learning and development, and belonging. It's not that everyone should get the same treatment, but that everyone has equal opportunities.

"This idea that for one stakeholder to win, another has to lose is bad design. I always think like a designer. Design is not the way something looks; design is how something works, and something works best when it works for the largest number of people," Airbnb CEO Brian Chesky told McKinsey.

When GitLab implemented "Async Weeks," an invitation for employees to clear their agendas and block time for deep work, they didn't anticipate the resistance from some groups. Client-facing employees such as sales and customer service don't have that freedom as they need to take care of external stakeholders. GitLab's culture team is currently exploring solutions for this challenge. In the meantime, they've encouraged sales and customer service employees to eliminate *internal* meetings.

Managing the complexities of scheduling, integrating individual and collective needs, and overseeing people who work from different locations isn't easy; having a centralized, top-down approach won't work. Team members can make better decisions when given freedom and authority.

It pays to keep your team rules simple and flexible and include team members in writing their own code of conduct. This is more than just a perk for employees; 72% of workers who are unhappy with their current level of flexibility are likely to look for a new job.[18] Flexibility is one of the best antidotes to the Great Resignation.

CAN YOU BUILD CULTURE REMOTELY? YES

The evidence is overwhelming. When done correctly, remote work increases productivity and work enjoyment. In addition, many professionals have experienced growth, both professionally and personally.

Additional research shows that over three-quarters of employees wish to work from home at least half of the time; almost 50% would rather quit their current job than not have the option to work remotely most of the time.[19]

Yet many leaders resist remote work and force employees to return to the office. Even Netflix's CEO wants people back in the physical workplace, despite not having an office himself.

So, why the disconnect?

I've spent a lot of time interviewing senior executives about this over the last few months. The recurring theme is that most CEOs believe their workplace culture has suffered during the pandemic, and they fear that it's impossible to keep it alive remotely. Senior leaders still believe that culture only happens in the office, requiring employees to see each other and have impromptu interactions and casual conversations.

While I agree that those elements are vital, they're not enough of an argument to bring people back into the office full-time.

This unfounded resistance is based on cognitive biases. On the one hand, the *safety bias* pushes executives to worry about the difficulties associated with working remotely. On the other hand, the *anchoring bias* promotes a faulty tendency—executives stay anchored to their past experiences and information.

There are many more biases in play as I observe working with different types of organizations.[20] But there's something else. Leaders feel powerless in a hybrid workplace. In short, they miss being in control.

Remote expert David Tate said it best: "When fearful CEOs talk about workplace culture, they're really talking about workplace control." Not all CEOs resist a hybrid workplace. Microsoft research shows that many value how flexibility can increase employee engagement. They also acknowledge the savings in office space and carbon footprint reduction; a hybrid environment means less commuting, reducing both vehicle and airline miles.

The fact remains, however, that not having employees at the office creates a perceived loss of control. Most leaders use visibility as a key performance indicator (KPI)—presentism, working long hours, or being in back-to-back meetings equal productivity.

Controlling leaders have become more controlling during the pandemic. That's why most people are overwhelmed. Remote work doesn't drive burnout, per se. It's leaders' desire to be in control that has added an unnecessary burden to people's workload.

Research shows that we are intrinsically motivated when we feel we have power over events in our lives. The pandemic disrupted this sentiment for everyone. It's natural for CEOs to feel lost, but letting go of control is vital to discover the upside of a hybrid workplace. Distance is not an obstacle but an opportunity to increase connection, collaboration, and agility.

Yes, you can build culture remotely.

It certainly requires a more concerted effort than in the office, but it's possible. In the following pages, I will share how companies such as Microsoft, GitLab, Volvo, Atlassian, Fannie Mae, Mars Wrigley, Slack, and many others are successfully building culture remotely. Moreover, I will dissect the principles behind successful cultures so you can design yours intentionally.

RESET CULTURE: WHERE TO START

What do I need to know to lead remotely?

Clients often ask me what tools they should be using. They think that thriving in a hybrid workplace is about logistics and technology. However, moving your culture in the right direction requires a new mindset, not just tools.

Leaders of hybrid teams will have to do what regional and global leaders have always done: work hard to create connections between on-site and remote employees.

Eliminating the labels that get in the way is a great way to start. As David Barker, Paddle's chief people officer, said, "We're trying to move away from labels right now; we like the idea of 'digital-first,' rather than being hybrid or remote teams or fully in the office. So how ever we operate, we want to operate in a digital way, meaning we capture things digitally and we're able to circulate [information] asynchronously."

Managing remotely is not the same as managing in the office. Unlearn what used to work. Here are some of the most significant adjustments you can make as you reset your culture for a hybrid/remote environment. If you are already practicing some of these, wonderful! The others should help you build on your efforts.

Let Go of Control; Become a Facilitator

When their teams went remote, many executives felt like they'd lost their superpowers. The authority of the corner office vanished almost overnight, becoming just another small rectangle in the Zoom grid view.

Leaders often resist a remote workplace, claiming that culture will be lost. In reality, they're afraid their charisma and influence might not be quite as important in a virtual setting. Or worse, maybe their contribution to culture wasn't as significant as they'd thought.

Resetting leadership starts by unlearning everything we know about how to lead. Rather than managing by watching (or, to paraphrase business guru Tom Peters, 'wandering around'), it's time to focus on facilitating the right system.

Few were trained or prepared to lead in a hybrid workplace, and this is actually an advantage as it opens up space for other voices. Instead of trying to drive the process, leaders have an opportunity to facilitate better conversations. Encourage people to ask better questions. Let them find the answers.

And listen.

How should we ask for help?
How can we have fun remotely?
How can we continually build trust remotely?
How can I help remove the corporate obstacles that get in the way?

Adapting to a remote-first environment is like visiting a foreign country. It requires learning a new language, behaviors, and culture. It's normal to feel disoriented.

Are you willing to embrace your vulnerability and say, "I don't know"? How do you feel about letting team members co-create the new culture rather than dictating the terms yourself? Are you open to maximizing the benefits of a remote environment even if it means your role feels less important?

Leading as a facilitator means letting go of the desire to be in charge and in control. Your role is to help your team decide on a shared future, facilitate ongoing conversations, and make sure no one is left behind.

The Office Is the New Offsite

The problem with the term "Zoom fatigue" is that we're blaming a tool instead of tackling a broken culture. Working from home is not the reason for burnout, but it has amplified existing problems within most organizations.

The truth is that the office isn't necessarily a great place to get work done.

As far back as 2013, the remote software company Basecamp's CEO, Jason Fried, argued that the modern office has become an *interruption factory* and claimed that "work doesn't happen at work."[21] The open office plan was meant to be a space for collaboration and transparency, but the reality was anything but ideal. Open offices are noisy, full of distractions, and lack privacy. Conflict ends up hidden behind closed doors.

Like it or not, the future of the workplace is no longer office-centric. Hacker One CEO Mårten Mickos agreed: "It's funny we call it the virtual world. We think it's something unnatural. However, civilization is flipping. The natural way will be [remote], and in-person will be the unusual one some years from now."[22]

The default is rapidly changing. Until recently, working from home was seen as the exception. Very soon, working from an office will be the exception.

It's time to rethink the office as the new offsite. It will become a space for special occasions, such as brainstorming, launching a new team, celebrating a big win, or running design sprints.

Clive Wilkinson Architects, the same company that created the open-office frenzy, has flipped its vision and is working on a new one.[23] Hint: It will include *the library*, a quiet space for deep work and research; *the plaza*, a kitchen and lunchroom to socialize with colleagues; and *the avenue*, a transitional space for passing with the potential for casual collaboration.

Supercharge the Trust Battery

Working in a hybrid environment requires trusting employees more than ever. This is critical for success.

Tobi Lütke, CEO of Shopify, popularized the idea of the trust battery.[24] He believes that when a new colleague joins your team, the trust battery between the two of you starts out at around 50%. Each time the new colleague acts in a positive way, the trust level increases, while negative behaviors decrease trust.

The trust battery is slow to charge yet quick to drain.

In most companies, you must earn trust over time to earn benefits, but in a remote environment, you don't have the luxury of time. A hybrid workplace demands that organizations take trust to a new level.

"Work appropriately" is GM's new norm to deal with hybrid work.[25] This play on the automaker's dress code ("Dress appropriately") promotes both trust and flexibility. Its approach acknowledges that the needs of each employee, project, and team are different.

The Australian software company Atlassian offers new employees a holiday before they even start working in the form of a travel voucher for a "holiday before you start."[26] This is more than just a perk; it's a clear message that Atlassian trusts its people. It's also an act of empathy: the company acknowledges that changing jobs is stressful.

Trust requires that someone take the first step. Leaders should be the first to demonstrate real trust in their employees. Fifty percent is not enough—they need to supercharge the trust battery. Thriving in a hybrid workplace requires trusting employees beyond what feels comfortable.

Virtual Friction Is Healthy

Conflict is a necessary force for growth. Teams that embrace tension, rather than run from it, are more successful. This is even truer in a remote environment.

When working in person, it's easy to spot signs that trouble is brewing. In a virtual space, signals are harder to read or confusing. The solution is to not only promote transparency but to encourage people to address conflict in the open.

GitLab, the poster child for remote work, believes that transparency is vital but not enough. GitLab prioritizes open discourse over private discourse. People must address conflict out in the open.

GitLab's solution is the "short toes" principle: no one should worry about stepping on someone else's toes because all employees have "short toes." Employees are encouraged to assume positive intent. If people say something that might feel uncomfortable, don't make it about yourself. Understand they want what's best for the company.

It's not easy, and leaders know that sometimes things can get ugly. However, a small dose of virtual friction is better than letting tensions fester.

Obsess over Communication

Employees usually do a lousy job of communicating in a physical space. We tend to infer a lot, talk in bullet points, and assume that everyone's taking note.

That's why Amazon has banned PowerPoint presentations and replaced them with the memo, a well-written document with real sentences. It provides a clear perspective about a topic with the background to make smart decisions.

The hybrid workplace requires a similar obsession with communication and documentation.

GitLab recommends a "handbook-first" approach, meaning they document everything in their handbook before it's even implemented.[27] Although this requires an up-front investment in time and effort, it pays off by reducing time, mistakes, and friction in the long run.

Documenting everything is about creating a *single source of truth*. Instead of asking people to come up with answers, you can look for the answer in the system itself. It saves time and headaches. Documentation also helps neutralize emotions. Instead of answers and solutions based on personal opinion, everyone is able to provide documentation in support of their ideas.

This kind of "curated conversation" is a powerful way to reduce conflict.

Leave No One Behind

One of the biggest challenges in a hybrid workplace is ensuring that those who work remotely are not left out of crucial conversations.

Proximity bias leads managers to favor those nearest them and who they see most often. On-site employees often have access to better perks, get more time with executives, and multiple studies show that those who are physically closer to managers are more likely to be promoted.[28] Remote employees, on the other hand, may be left out of decision-making, ignored on calls, and even paid less.

This bias is almost always unconscious, which is why it's so dangerous.

The solution lies in first letting go of the idea that being at the office makes people more productive. Recall Mindset Shift #2, From Input to Impact. Leaders need to make a conscious effort to include everyone and to evaluate people based on goals and results, not on time spent. Leaders also need to ensure that all voices are heard.

Below are some ways to make this shift a reality.

Level the playing field

Look for ways that you can create the same—or, at least, a similar—experience for everyone. For example, if you happen to work from the office, show empathy by designing a hybrid experience rather than expecting remote attendees to adapt to you.

At Trello, if even one person joins a meeting remotely, everyone else joins from their desks. This creates a similar experience for all attendees so that no one feels like they're at a disadvantage. They want to empathize with others to encourage balanced participation.

Microsoft usually selects a facilitator who's not in the room to run hybrid meetings, and everyone follows a set of rules that levels the playing field. If anyone wants to ask a question, they have to raise their hands, either physically or virtually. All team members join via Microsoft Teams regardless of whether they are in the room or participating from home. The chat function is used by everyone to ask questions or share additional information.

Share the pain of the remote jet lag

Traditionally, time zone differences created a lot of friction among team members. According to a study by Google, remote team members always had to adapt to the "central office" time, sometimes having to attend meetings very early or very late in the day.[29]

We all need to be more aware and adapt. After realizing the effort many participants were making to join my workshops at, for them, weird hours, I decided to share the pain and offer alternative times to make it easier for people to participate. Now sometimes, it's me who suffers from virtual jet lag, kicking off a workshop at five a.m. my time, or finishing at ten p.m.

This experience has made me more conscious than ever of the challenges of time zones. We all need to adjust and make sure that everyone gets *their* turn to attend at regular hours.

Be more inclusive

Part of the reason that people don't want to go back to offices is that often, offices weren't inclusive spaces to begin with, particularly for people from underrepresented backgrounds, for introverts, and for new employees.

Working from home has blurred the boundaries between home and work, making it more difficult for women, in particular, to switch off. According to the Women at Work survey in 2021, 65% of working women felt the pandemic made things worse for them.[30]

Balancing work and family obligations has become an uphill battle, especially for mothers who lack child care or workplace support. These factors have led to women feeling less ambitious about their careers. The majority feel burned out, and more than one-third said they've thought about quitting over the past year.

Despite these challenges, women showed up as better leaders during the pandemic, providing emotional support to their team members and championing diversity, equity, and inclusion (DEI).[31] However, their dedication has not been reciprocated by their (mostly male) managers. Even worse, all that extra work is unrecognized, underappreciated, and won't lead to career advancement.

A hybrid work environment requires being more intentional about inclusion and equal participation. Leaders must ensure no one is left behind.

Recap

STEP 1: RESET YOUR CULTURE

A hybrid workplace is here to stay.

Thriving in the environment requires revisiting (almost) everything about your company culture.

Successful remote-first organizations design their culture intentionally and obsessively.

Despite the concerns of some leaders, it is possible to successfully build a remote culture.

Leaders must "unlearn" traditional leadership strategies and design an equal experience for both remote and on-site employees.

YOUR TURN:
RESET YOUR CULTURE

The Culture Reset Canvas is a simple tool for facilitating crucial conversations about what's working and what isn't. More importantly, it's an invitation to design the future, leverage the good practices you should preserve, and shed the less helpful ones.

In this facilitation guide, I explain how to manage the conversation and provide a list of questions that spark great conversations.

You can facilitate this conversation in person, remotely, or use a combination of both. I recommend using MURAL or another virtual whiteboard to provide a space for everyone to share their thoughts and capture the agreements.

A facilitator should manage turn-taking and guarantee equal participation. Remember that the quality of a culture reset depends on the quality of the questions. Ask the right ones and let the conversation flow. Just listen. Open-ended questions invite dialogue and elicit more information than simply assigning a score to a statement.

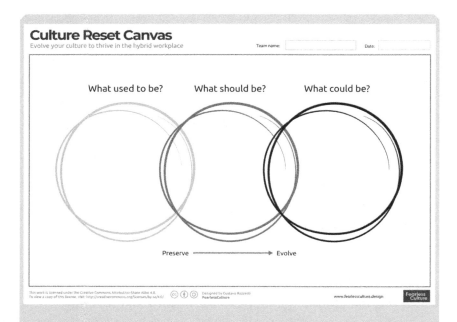

Begin by downloading a copy of the Culture Reset Canvas using the QR code below.

The tool has three circles, each of which represents a crucial question:

- What used to be?
- What should be?
- What could be?

Kickoff (10-15 minutes)

Introduce the goal of the session and the Culture Reset Canvas framework.

Start with a quick check-in round or facilitate an icebreaker. For example, inviting team members to share "I'm amazing because… " is an excellent way to reinforce interpersonal relationships and kick off with an appreciative mindset.

Define and share the ground rules to promote a safe, collaborative space. The success of the session depends on openness and active participation.

What Used to Be? (30-45 minutes)

In this part, you want to capture two things:

- Your culture pre-pandemic
- Your culture once people were forced to work from home

Differentiating between the two will help you understand what was working in the past, what stopped working in the new reality, and what improvements your team has made.

Use the following questions to inspire a richer discussion:

- What do you love most about this team?
- What brought you here and what has motivated you to stay?
- What do you value most about your team members?
- What gives/gave life to our organization?
- What were our highs and lows? What has driven each?
- What are the core factors behind our success? And the ones that get us stuck?
- When we played at our best, what did you see, who was involved, how did we make decisions, and what were our strengths? (Repeat for when we played at our worst).
- Think about a story of overcoming a challenge that makes you feel proud of this team. What happened? What was the obstacle? What enabled us to succeed?

Begin by letting each person capture their ideas in silence.

Next, have everyone share one thought at a time. If some-one has already shared a similar thought, people can say they agree but should try to contribute a new idea.

Group similar ideas and find a theme that best describes the cluster. Avoid focusing on just the most common topics; a crucial issue might be brought up by only one team member.

What Should Be? (15-30 minutes)

Review all the groups and discuss which elements of culture you want to preserve and which you want to discard.

Use the following prompts to facilitate the discussion:

- What are the key themes behind our success?
- What mindsets and practices from our past were vital to adapt to WFH?
- What mindsets and practices from the past got in the way in a WFH/ distributed workplace?
- Which practices and mindsets from the past should we keep?
- What are the things that no longer serve the team?
- In what areas did we make a lot of improvements (collaboration, feedback, psychological safety, meetings, etc.)?
- What contributed the most for us to successfully adapt to the new reality?
- Who helped you the most and why?
- What new behaviors and practices have we adopted during the pandemic that we should preserve?

Not everything you want to get rid of will be "bad." Some processes or behaviors might have worked in the past but no longer serve the team in a hybrid workplace. These are the hardest to spot and let go of.

The team must be aligned in what they want to preserve and get rid of before moving to the next step. If participants get stuck, the facilitator can use the consent process to unlock the discussion.

What Could Be? (30-45 minutes)

The third part is about imagining a better future.

Start by inviting team members to dream about what the future could look like. Encourage them to imagine they're doing the best work of their lives.

- What are they doing? With whom? And how?
- In this exciting future, how do we operate as a team?
- What defines a role model in our team?
- What behaviors and mindsets make us proud?
- What systems and methods help us do better work?
- What communication structures are in place?
- How do we hold each other accountable and support one another?

Allow a couple of minutes for everyone to dream on their own and then share their vision of the future. The team should agree on a shared future.

Capture the behaviors and practices from the second circle that will help you get there. Identify which need to be evolved/adapted and which will continue to work as is. What's missing?

Design the elements of culture that need to be incorporated to help your team achieve your dream future.

Wrap up the session by creating an action plan of who will do what and when.

REIMAGINE
A SHARED FUTURE

STEP 2

When famed anthropologist Margaret Mead was asked what she considered to be the first sign of civilization, her reply took her students by surprise. She didn't mention religious artifacts, clay pots, or grinding stones. Instead, she pointed to a 15,000-year-old human femur that had been broken and healed.

Mead explained that if an animal breaks its leg, it will certainly die. No creature can run from danger, hunt for food, or seek out fresh water with a broken leg. There's not enough time for the broken bone to heal; a predator will eat it first. A broken leg bone that has healed is evidence that a human being stopped what they were doing and took care of the wounded person until the bone healed.

"Helping someone else through difficulty is where civilization starts," Mead concluded.

This definition of civilization is an important reminder of something we tend to forget: human nature is inherently good and helpful. People don't just want a job; they want to create a positive impact that goes beyond the organization they work for.

Normally, we associate successful organizations with a strong product, technology, or leader, but it's the organizations with a strong sense of purpose—the ones that have created a shared future that includes everyone—that usually end up leaders in their industries.

Successful teams don't just work together; their members care for each other. Collaboration and alignment are by-products of culture. Team members help and support each other because they share a future. They know that their mission can only be accomplished if they work together. Unfortunately, most organizations fail to align their team members. They focus on the *what* (the goals, tasks, or activities) rather than on the *why* (the purpose).

A shared purpose brings clarity and focus, especially in times of crisis. That's why some organizations thrived during the pandemic while most struggled. Unilever, Patagonia, Gravity Payments, and Airbnb, to name a few, were forced to making tough decisions when COVID-19 hit, yet they flourished where others failed.

Now, as companies increasingly move to hybrid work, a clear purpose becomes more vital than ever, serving as a kind of North Star that keeps employees aligned in the service of a shared future, regardless of how distant they are from each other.

Step 2: Reimagine a Shared Future, is about driving alignment by focusing on creating a positive impact. I will discuss what purpose is, why it matters, and how to create one for your team.

WHAT PURPOSE IS (AND ISN'T)

"Purpose" is more than just a way to inspire your employees. Being a purpose-driven organization runs much deeper than that, and it's not always easy. Anyone can *say* they have a purpose; your actions are what make it real.

Ever since Simon Sinek delivered his now-famous 2010 TED Talk, "Start with Why," having a company purpose statement has become something of a fad. Most of the time, purpose statements end up being just inspirational quotes, more window dressing than a real commitment to make tough choices.

This misses the point entirely. Being a purpose-driven organization is not about having a feel-good culture; it's about creating alignment among your employees and teams and helping to solve complex problems. A shared future ensures that every member of the company is on the same page with regard to short-term and long-term business initiatives, workflow, and expectations.

And the benefits of a strong purpose aren't limited to smoother workflow. According to consulting firm EY, purpose-driven companies succeed at driving innovation and transformational change.[32] While 84% of executives say that having purpose increases their ability to transform, 80% say it also helps increase customer loyalty.

Before we go deeper into what a purpose is, it's worth pointing out that it shouldn't be confused with your mission or vision statements.[33]

Briefly, a *mission* statement is a straightforward description of what an organization does. It might include the type of product or services it delivers, its primary customers or market, where it operates, and its main competitive advantages.

A *vision* statement describes what the organization wishes to be like in the future. Company visions are often ego-focused; leaders puff out their chests with terms like "best in class," "desire to win," or "biggest."

A well-defined purpose statement, on the other hand, is about serving others—not yourself and not your company. It is people-focused, more reflective, connected, and human. Tesla's purpose, for example, is "To accelerate the world's transition to sustainable energy." It doesn't say anything about being the most innovative electric car company, the market leader, or creating the latest technology. Tesla's purpose is about the impact the company wants to create.

Your purpose should express itself in your company's actions. When CVS decided to stop selling tobacco products, most people thought the company was crazy; tobacco-related sales were worth $2 billion annually. But the message was loud and clear: the company wanted to be consistent with its purpose, "Helping people on their path to better health."

Putting purpose ahead of profit proved to be the right call. CVS not only stayed true to its promise, but it transformed people's behavior for the better. Its customers became 38% more likely to stop buying cigarettes altogether. The retailer even managed to offset the short-term loss and continue growing.[34]

Facebook, on the other hand, has *not* consistently stood by its purpose, which is "To give people the power to share and make the world more open and connected." Based on the recent backlash around fake news, propaganda, and hate speech, however, Facebook is less concerned with making the world more connected than it is with making more revenue, regardless of the damage it causes. The social media company is not taking a real stand.

 Having a purpose is more than a company motto. It requires authenticity and commitment. A purpose is your guidepost; it guides people's behavior, especially during difficult times. Your purpose is the reason why people want to work together, collaborate, and achieve a shared goal. It's the single underlying *raison d'être* that brings all stakeholders together.

Put simply, your purpose defines your "why."

WHY DOES YOUR COMPANY EXIST?

A common purpose helps create a sense of belonging and makes people more productive and engaged. This is a win-win for both the individual and the organization. But it's also the key to other elements of your culture.

A few years ago, Airbnb's founders had an epiphany. They realized they stood for something more than just places for people to stay. As a result, they evolved the company's purpose to reflect why the company exists: "Create a world where anyone can belong anywhere."

Airbnb exists to provide travel experiences that are local, authentic, diverse, inclusive, and sustainable. The company believes that everyone should be able to take the perfect trip, and that where they stay, what they do, and who they meet is part of that.

Brian Chesky, Airbnb's CEO, expressed a clear commitment to the company's purpose: "The rules of business have changed. The best thing for shareholders is for society to want us to exist. And society will want us to exist if they think that as Airbnb benefits, they benefit."

When the pandemic hit, travel, of course, came to a halt, and Airbnb had to let almost 25% of its workforce go. The leadership didn't take that decision lightly, as you can read in Chesky's open letter to all employees.[35]

Not only did Airbnb's CEO choose to be open and candid, but he was also humble and caring. Rather than delegating the task to HR, he shared the bad news himself. He acted like a great host, treating employees as if they belonged even if they had to part ways. Airbnb offered a severance package, reducing caps so everyone could claim their equity shares and prolonging health benefits, and it created an Alumni Talent Directory to help people find new jobs.

When confronted with a difficult situation, Airbnb acted in accordance with its purpose. There's a difference between having a purpose and using your purpose as a real North Star. Chesky reflected: "In a crisis, you have three choices. You could do less than is expected of you, you can do what is expected of you, or you can do more than is expected of you. A crisis is a spotlight. It's a moment to demonstrate your values and lead by example."

Companies, of course, change over time, and as your company evolves, your purpose should evolve with it.

Many people use the purpose of the outdoor clothing and gear company Patagonia, "We are in business to save the planet," as a model and encourage companies to adopt something equally high-minded. They don't always realize, however, that Patagonia's current purpose has evolved over decades of work. The company's previous purpose was solid if a little less inspiring: "Build the best product, cause no unnecessary harm, use business to inspire, and implement solutions to the environmental crisis."

Over time, the company has gone from demonstrating a quiet commitment to the environment to full-on activism. In 2017, Patagonia sued the US government in an effort to protect national parks. It made another bold move in 2018 by endorsing two US Senate candidates who vowed to protect public lands.[36]

Patagonia's purpose—and actions—show a real commitment to saving planet Earth.

Not all company purposes need to be as altruistic as Patagonia's, although that would be fantastic. However, your purpose should capture your contribution to making the world better. Note that "world" can refer to your immediate community, city, or country. It doesn't have to be the entire planet.

IAG's purpose is focused on helping its customers. The Australian insurance company exists "To help people manage risk and recover from the hardship of unexpected loss." Although it might feel less ambitious than Patagonia's, IAG provides a positive impact—to alleviate the suffering of its customers during hard times.

Daniel Pink, the author of *Drive*, defines purpose "as the yearning to do work in the service of something larger than ourselves." People want more than just a paycheck. Working toward something that matters is the highest form of motivation.

WHY A TEAM PURPOSE MATTERS

One of the biggest challenges that companies face while working remotely is keeping their employees engaged, connected, and aligned. This brings me to the topic of subcultures. In addition to sharing the company's main culture, successful teams have strong subcultures, too.

 Some people confuse subcultures with silos. They are similar, but not the same.

All silos are subcultures, but not all subcultures are silos. Organizational silos happen when a specific team or area doesn't want to collaborate with others, keeping information, secrets, and knowledge to themselves. A healthy subculture has a strong identity, but it's not disconnected. Company culture and team subcultures nourish and support each other.

Research shows that when people have a stronger connection to their team, they are 2.3 times more likely to be fully engaged.[37]

People like to be part of a tribe, and the smaller the group, the stronger the affiliation. This sense of belonging, as I will cover in Step 3, is critical to bringing remote team members together.

Team members have more frequent interaction among themselves than with people from outside their "tribe." This has been magnified since teams went remote. Remote work isolated teams, but also led to more intense communication within smaller groups, as a study of 360 billion emails shows.[38]

A team purpose helps align its members by providing a reason for why the team exists and why it wants to accomplish its goals. It provides direction to the team subculture while connecting it with the company's purpose.

Team members want to be part of something larger and more important than themselves. Research shows that 76% of employees crave a sense of purpose.[39] A clear purpose increases motivation and engagement, and improving team culture can drive faster results than fixing the overall culture.[40] Despite that, however, teams are often busy delivering their work with little idea of why they're doing it.

Most importantly, a team purpose drives fulfillment. It helps connect people to their personal purpose, aligning them with who they are, their gifts, and their desire to have meaningful lives.

Designing a team purpose helps define a shared future; it gives clarity, enhances motivation, and drives people into action. It connects team members with a sense of meaning by addressing three critical questions:

- What do we do?
- Who do we work for?
- What is the impact that we want to create?

Having a team purpose complements organizational purpose. It helps translate the overarching "why" into a simpler, closer, and more relatable version. It connects the team members' everyday activities to the bigger company picture and clarifies how a specific team will enable the organization to achieve its goals.

The Alignment/Autonomy Grid

Source: Henrik Kniberg/Spotify—Aligned Autonomy

The alignment/autonomy grid, shown above, perfectly captures Spotify's approach to team alignment.

When autonomy is high but alignment is low, the result is busy but chaotic, with teams running around in different directions with no clear sense of an overall goal.

When alignment is high but autonomy is low, workers will get the job done as a result of top-down directives, but they're unlikely to feel a sense of personal engagement or responsibility. They're "just doing their jobs."

And when alignment and autonomy are both low, the result is confusion and apathy. Very little gets done, and no one takes responsibility for anything.

However, when alignment and autonomy are both high, leaders can align teams around a common mission and then let them figure out the solution. Spotify's leaders don't ask teams to build a bridge. Instead, they give them the mission—"we must cross the river"—and let them figure out how to accomplish it.

This is a great reminder that having a clear purpose can drive team alignment and inspire the team to create the solution rather than having it dictated by their boss.

Creating a Shared Future

Typically, companies have a purpose, but their teams don't. This provides an opportunity to develop yours. And even if your team has a purpose, the new reality of hybrid work makes it imperative to revisit it.

 Alignment doesn't mean consensus, nor does it require that team members agree on everything. However, we want the team to co-create the future they want together.

The journey of designing a shared future can be as rewarding as the destination itself. In my experience of helping teams develop their purpose, the conversations and debates that this exercise spark are both enlightening and transformational.

Mars Wrigley's global packaging leadership team started working together one year into the pandemic. Most of the members hadn't had the chance to meet each other in person. Although the team was doing great and lots of initiatives were moving forward, there was some connection missing and boundaries weren't always respected.

As part of a consulting project with Mars Wrigley, I facilitated several workshops to help the team increase belonging and psychological safety in a remote setting and, most importantly, to reset its culture for a hybrid environment. The team purpose design part, however, was the most transformational.

At first, most members didn't think that having a team purpose statement would change much. However, as we went through different iterations—and with some pushback from their leader—the conversation went to a different level. The team got into interesting debates about who they really served, unearthing differences and unaddressed tensions. Many people felt their role was to serve internal clients, like regional managers, the innovation team, or even the CEO. However, the most profound shift came once they realized that their work made the biggest impact on the consumer. They decided to focus on the consumer in the future by "making the product experience more meaningful."

William Singleton, director global packaging development, told me: "It was a great experience articulating our team purpose and spending time to map our objectives to the purpose. I don't recall doing that before. In a distributed team, it's crucial to pause and reflect on why we are doing what we are doing."

WHEN THE GOING GETS TOUGH, PURPOSE MATTERS

Nothing reveals your culture like a crisis. Your culture's true nature is exposed by the decisions your company makes under pressure. And the greater the pressure, the more your company's purpose is put to the test.

At the end of 2019, Glassdoor predicted that 2020 would be the decade of culture-first organizations. Then came the coronavirus pandemic.

As people and businesses faced the biggest economic challenge of their lives, the need for survival forced leaders to make tough choices—should we stay true to who we are or just focus on keeping our heads above water?

Even under the best of circumstances, no one enjoys uncertainty, and it can be very tempting to take the most expedient route. That route, however, should never come at the expense of long-term values. Employees may lower their expectations temporarily to keep their jobs, but they won't forget how organizations treat them when things get back to "normal." The Great Resignation that we're experiencing now didn't happen overnight; it was years in the making.

Following are three things purpose guides you to do, keeping you true to yourself, especially in times of crisis.

Do the Right Thing

Having a company purpose statement has become almost de rigueur, but much of the time, it's just an inspirational phrase that has little real impact. Ultimately, an organization's purpose is defined by its actions, not its words.

Basecamp made a strong statement in the spring of 2020 when it stood up against employee surveillance. Third-party developers were using its API to develop software that recorded and monitored remote workers' activities.

Basecamp's revised policy stated:

> *"We're about remote work within an environment of trust, not spying on your employees. It's recently come to our attention that some third-party integrations go beyond traditional time tracking functionality to surveillance. We're not okay with that, and we're codifying that stance in this policy update."*

Basecamp chose doing the right thing over revenue—right in line with its stated value of "Be fair and do the right thing."[41]

Starbucks did the same when it announced in March 2020 that it would cancel seating in its cafés to encourage social distancing, modeling its value of "acting with courage, challenging the status quo." Starbuck CEO Kevin Johnson explained that the company was adapting as new information was made available, making choices that felt right for its employees and customers, not just the business.

Are your decisions aligned with your company's purpose?

Put People First

People want to be treated as human beings, not resources, especially in times of crisis, and they should be able to expect their organizations to support them. Leaders should provide a sense of solidarity. Occasionally, that may call for radical openness.

Gravity's CEO Dan Price had to choose between laying off 20% of his workforce or going bankrupt. Rather than making the call on his own, he presented his employees with the harsh truth and asked them for ideas. Together, they decided that each person would take a salary cut depending on what they could afford. This collective, flexible response helped the company adapt and avoid both bankruptcy and layoffs.[42]

Several other companies stepped up to take care of their employees during the early days of the pandemic. Columbia Sportswear reduced the salary of its chief executive to $10,000 a year, and at least ten executives took a voluntary 15% pay cut. This allowed the company to continue paying its 3,500 US employees who couldn't work in its shuttered stores. This unusual decision put employees, not senior executives, first.

Several other organizations, including Morgan Stanley, PayPal, Starbucks, and Bank of America, suspended layoffs during the pandemic.[43]

According to Jeffrey Pfeffer, this kind of altruism didn't happen during the 2009 recession. The Stanford University professor told *The Washington Post* by reducing uncertainty and financial stress, people would be grateful, more loyal, and work harder.[44]

Organizations that put people first during the global pandemic will be rewarded in the long run. Research by Ozlem Brooke Erol, founder of Purposeful Business, shows that purpose-driven companies have been resilient during the pandemic. Not only did they continue to grow, they have also been less affected by the Great Resignation.

Take Care of the Community

It's easy to be true to your purpose during normal times, but a crisis that reduces sales and profit puts your organization's values to the test. Do you exist just to make money, or to also create a positive impact in the world?

It was comforting to see how many companies stepped up and retooled their operations to take care of the community in the face of the pandemic—not because they had to, but because they wanted to.

Nordstrom, the luxury clothing department store, is the single largest employer of tailors in the US.[45] When the face mask shortage became public, its alteration teams decided to take action—they took on a mission to sew nearly one million masks to be distributed to frontline health care workers across two major hospital networks.[46]

Nordstrom believes its most important responsibility as a company is giving back to the diverse communities it serves. Gigi Ganatra, VP of corporate affairs and public relations, explained. "While this is something that we do year-round, in times of emergency, this belief takes on an even bigger responsibility, and in this case, a global one."

When the Leesa Sleep team heard there was a potential lack of one-quarter of a million hospital beds, they wanted to do something about it. Leesa's products are not suited for hospitals, so the team had to develop a new bed—and that's what they did—in less than three weeks.[47] Leesa's team created a bed with suitable elevation for COVID-19 patients in record time.

Leading through purpose will not only help your employees and community but also your business. Purpose-oriented companies have higher productivity and growth rates. Research by Deloitte shows that purpose-driven organizations are 30% more innovative and their employees are 40% more loyal.[48]

Build something lasting. Make decisions that count. You might feel the pressure all around you; the pandemic (or whatever crisis comes next) state of mind will tempt you to take the easiest path. As a leader, you can make a difference in the lives of others.

Forget short-term thinking. Focus on real impact.

CULTURE IS THE BEHAVIOR YOU REWARD AND PUNISH

Workplace culture is more than "the way we do things around here." It's the gap between what we say and what we do. It's the behavior that is tolerated, not your words, that determines the real culture.

 Company values are invisible. What's rewarded and punished shouldn't be.

Marc Eugenio found an angel on Christmas Eve. The US Bank customer was stranded. He had been waiting for hours for a deposit to show up in his account, but his bank balance—and fuel tank—were still empty.

After a long call with customer service, a representative offered to hand Mr. Eugenio $20 of her own money. Emily James, a senior US Bank officer, received permission from her manager and drove to meet the customer during her lunchtime. She handed him the money and wished Marc a Merry Christmas.

You would think the employer would reward Emily for her selfless behavior, right? Not so fast.

Rather than acknowledging her generous behavior, US Bank accused Emily of putting the bank at unnecessary risk because she'd broken a company rule that bars call center employees from meeting customers. It fired both her and her manager.[49]

Interesting response from a company that empowers employees to "do the right thing."

The Problem with Company Values

Sadly, the above story is the norm rather than the exception.

As a culture consultant, I often observe this disconnect between the declared culture and the real one. Corporate behaviors don't match words.

Almost one-third of employees in the UK feel their organization's vision or values have too much corporate jargon, and 49% can't recite their organization's values.[50] In the US, more than 30% of employees believe business leaders don't behave in ways that are consistent with the company's stated values.[51]

Take Boeing as an example. Integrity, trust, and safety, among others, are the aerospace company's core values. However, an analysis of recent safety incidents unearthed the real behavior. Boeing's company culture is anything but safe. Employees neither trust each other nor respect its safety approach—engineers are even called "clowns."[52]

A lack of consistency between words and action is also a common issue when crafting company values. Despite adopting the mantra "Don't Be Evil" as part of its company code of conduct, it appears Google *is* guilty of being evil now and again. Recently, three former employees sued the company for wrongfully terminating their contracts. They spoke out about Google's pursuit of controversial projects with the US government, including customer surveillance.

Patrick Lencioni, the author of *The Advantage*, identified four types of company values, listed below.[53]

Core values are the principles that guide your company's behavior. They cannot be compromised. Not only are they deeply ingrained in the organization, but they also make your culture unique. Core values capture shared beliefs—what's expected of people in your company. If purpose provides the *why* for your company, core values provide the *how*.

Airbnb CEO Chesky, says it best: "Integrity, honesty—those aren't core values. Those are values that everyone should have. But there have to be like three, five, six things that are unique to you."[54]

Aspirational values are those the company needs but currently lacks. Aspirational values can be deceiving. The fact that you add them to your list doesn't mean that you actually live them. They require turning words into action.

Taken too far, aspirational values can be harmful, especially if there's a lack of context or role modeling. For example, "be brutally honest" can promote disrespect or lack of compassion for our colleagues.[55]

Permission-to-play values are the minimum expected behavior of any employee, regardless of their job. They don't differ from one company to another. "Collaboration," "integrity," or "diversity," to name a few, are not core values; they're the bare minimum of acceptable behavior.

So, why do organizations insist on including these bare minimums as values? Usually to get out of trouble. Netflix added the "Diversity" value to its culture map after experiencing backlash.[56] Similarly, when Uber refreshed its values, it included "Do the right thing. Period" as part of an effort to neutralize an incredibly toxic culture.[57]

Last, **accidental values** happen organically and grow over time. Sometimes they are company values taken to an extreme (such as when "work hard" becomes "work to the point of exhaustion"). Other times, they reflect employees' interests and aspirations. Sometimes they elevate the culture but usually, they don't.

The problem with values is that most leaders fall in love with their own words. They like to craft a self-serving purpose statement but fail to distinguish their aspirations from reality.

Actions speak louder than words

"So what should I do to get ahead in your organization? What makes people successful here? What made you successful?"

Charles O'Reilly, co-director of the Stanford Graduate School of Business, posed that question and invited VMware's employees to reflect on what the company rewarded.[58] Employees started filling the board with the usual suspects—innovate, work hard, be open, and be collaborative. But with prompting, more specific behaviors started to appear: "Be available on email 24x7," "Sound smart," and "Get consensus on your decisions." Once the team had finished, professor O'Reilly pointed at the whiteboard and said, "That's your culture. Your culture is the behaviors you reward and punish."

The discussion about the behaviors that are rewarded and punished is much harder than it seems and leaders often struggle with this exercise. Listing values is easy; connecting them to actual behaviors is a different story.

Research indicates that stated values often don't have a significant impact and can even have a negative effect. An MIT Sloan study found no correlation between a company's expressed values and how employees felt they lived up to them.[59] For example, promoting diversity but not supporting it with action can do more harm than good.[60] Statements such as "We don't discriminate" create an impression that the organization has achieved equity and fairness when, in fact, it hasn't.

Behavioral cues, on the other hand, provide concrete guidance on how to translate values into actions. Leaders must clarify why they matter. According to the same study by MIT, less than one-quarter of companies connect values with behaviors, and a significant majority fail to link beliefs with business success.

 You can't call your culture "transparent" if people are afraid of speaking truth to power. You can't say you have a "collaborative" workplace if you regularly promote selfish employees. You can't pronounce your culture "innovative" if breakthrough ideas are often killed before they see the light of day.

US Bank cannot say that it wants employees to "Do the right thing" and then fire an employee who did a good deed.

Company culture is a reflection of its leaders—not just what they do but also what they tolerate. To change your company's culture, seek to change which behaviors you celebrate or call out. Your actions—or lack thereof—speak louder than a thousand words. Anish Hindocha, change lead at ITV told me, "What you ignore, disregard, turn a blind eye to, or sweep under a carpet becomes the things you implicitly endorse."[61]

It is also is worth noting that it's what employees *think* you punish and reward that matters. Emmett Shear, CEO of Twitch, tweeted: "Your culture is determined by what people *perceive* to be the behaviors you reward and punish. Note: Not what you *actually* reward and punish and also not what you *say* you reward and punish."[62] (Italics mine.)

Letting an underperforming employee go is difficult and painful. You invested a lot in hiring them and you want them to succeed. However, delaying the decision can send the wrong message. People could think that bad performance is okay.

Defining the behaviors you want to reward and punish is not about building consensus but about drawing a line. Choose what's right, not what's easy.

Some examples:

Amazon punishes "complacency" and having a "Day 2 mentality." Mediocrity is not welcomed. The tech giant rewards speed, relentlessness, and intellectual autonomy. This is consistent with Amazon's aggressive culture.[63]

HubSpot punishes taking shortcuts to achieve short-term results. Conversely, it rewards simplicity, being a "culture-add" (someone who actively improves the company), work and life balance, and results delivered, not hours worked.

Spotify punishes playing politics. Instead, it rewards creativity. Ideas—not the person with the highest pay grade—win.

Slack punishes "brilliant jerks." There's no room for people who are disrespectful or not team players. Instead, Slack rewards empathy, a characteristic that's crucial to getting a job at the tech company.

Culture is how people behave when no one is looking

Culture is not your company brand or the speech you give at an all-hands meeting. Your culture is actual day-to-day behavior. It's the tough choices you make to stay true to your purpose and values, from dealing with mistakes or bad news to establishing why people get promoted or fired.

Ozlem Brooke Erol told me: "Doing the right thing for the wrong reasons doesn't work. People can tell the difference. A purpose is not a tagline—you can't ask a marketing agency to develop it, you have to live your purpose."

Erol shared the story of TRU Colors, whose purpose is to "Brew opportunity and end gang violence." This brewing company from North Carolina is taking action for social change. Not only does it educate people through conversations, it also provides job opportunities, mentoring, and educational programs.

TRU Colors was created by George Taylor after a 16-year-old boy was killed in a shooting near his office. Taylor built a business with a fully integrated social mission. The CEO is using beer as a conduit for social change. If beer brings people together, why not use it to create a community hub and social space?

 Your true culture happens when no one is watching—it's the result of what gets rewarded or punished.

Viisi is a Dutch mortgage advisory firm on a mission to change finance. Its purpose is to make the finance industry better, more sustainable, and more focused on the long-term. Tom van der Lubbe cofounded Viisi based on the idea that something was missing in his previous corporate job.

The financial industry is difficult, according to van der Lubbe—it doesn't treat society well. He believes Viisi should advise people so that 25 years from now, their mortgage decisions will still make sense. The CEO decided to change the usual order, putting people first, clients second, and shareholders last.

This "people-first" standard works on the principle that if employees are motivated and happy, they will do the best for clients. And if clients are happy, the business will grow, thus delivering sustainable gains to stakeholders.

Viisi results show that being purpose-driven pays off. Not only has the company continued to grow, even during the pandemic, but its customers have given the company an average rating of 9.8 out of 10.

Model the right behavior and inspire others to follow suit. Walk the talk. Let your actions, not your words, define your culture. What you reward and punish requires drawing a line—how far are you willing to go to protect your culture?

PRIORITIES: GOOD > GOOD

Leadership is the art of making decisions. Saying "yes" is easy, but what we say "no" to defines our success, especially when we have to choose between two good things. Great leaders know when to make sacrifices to stay focused.

Imagine taking over a tech company that's hemorrhaging money because sales are down. Would you choose to launch more products or cut the innovation pipeline by 70%?

That's the dilemma Steve Jobs was faced with when he returned to Apple in 1997. The company's sales had plummeted 30% during the final quarter of 1996. Apple was on the brink of failure.

Jobs would eventually turn the company he founded around, but only after he had made some tough decisions. Jobs reduced the number of Apple products by 70% and focused on producing only four products: the Power Macintosh G3 desktop, the PowerBook G3 portable computer for professionals, the iMac desktop, and iBook portable computer for consumers.

Jobs said, "Deciding what not to do is as important as deciding what to do. It's true for companies, and it's true for products."[64] He understood that prioritization is all about making tough calls, especially when it requires favoring one good thing over another good thing.

It was a tough choice, but it paid off. During Jobs's first fiscal year, Apple lost $1.04 billion and was 90 days from being insolvent. One year later, the company made a $309 million profit.

Prioritization is not limited to strategic business decisions, such as the product innovation pipeline. What you choose—or don't—is crucial to designing your workplace culture, too. Having analyzed hundreds of workplace cultures, I've found that thriving ones have one thing in common: clear priorities. Successful company cultures are crystal clear about what's important to them; they know what they say "no" to. That's why they're less interested in attracting the best talent than in attracting the talent that's right for them.

 When an organization says "yes" to everything, they are saying "no" to what really matters. Patagonia founder Yvon Chouinard said it best: "The sooner a company tries to be what it is not, the sooner it tries to have it all, the sooner it will die."

Prioritization is more than just focusing; it's about staying true to what an organization stands for——its purpose and values. A great approach to establishing clear organizational priorities is to use a set of "even over" statements. They help clarify decision-making.

An "even over" statement is a declaration of priority. You are saying that you will prioritize one good thing *even over* another good thing. Your team will become what they focus on. Even over statements resolve the conflict when dealing with two good things and make it easier for employees to think for themselves without having to consult their manager.

Here are some examples of even over statements:

- Employees' happiness, even over customers' happiness
- Speed, even over perfection
- High performance, even over harmony

When Netflix prioritizes "performance even over effort," it doesn't mean that the company doesn't care about the employees giving all they've got. It means that Netflix cares more about the result than the effort itself.

Likewise, "Long-term vision even over quick wins" captures Airbnb's relentless focus on long-term success. It doesn't mean that the company doesn't seize quick wins under the right circumstances, but that Airbnb won't do anything that could jeopardize its vision, such as resisting the temptation of scale and speed to make sure they hire the right people.

Defining even over statements doesn't mean that one thing isn't good, it's simply that there's a better choice. Prioritization requires sacrifice, but it encourages us to make clear choices.

PRIORITIES IN A HYBRID WORLD

A hybrid working environment creates additional tensions between what individuals want and what's possible. Defining priorities in advance can help minimize conflict and simplify decision-making.

Here are some examples of priorities that address common tensions affecting hybrid teams:

- Outcome, even over effort
- Personal needs, even over team preferences
- Team members' well-being, even over productivity

Outcome, even over effort

It's easy for culture to get diluted if a company is working remotely—and especially when it's growing fast. To keep its values front center, GitLab's CEO Sid Sijbrandij made a commitment to codify its values, regularly update them, and find new ways to bring them to life.

The company makes its values public to show respect for job seekers. It gives people the opportunity to see if they share those same values before interviewing. However, Sijbrandij understands that not all their values are equal, so he's established a hierarchy. "Results" is at the top, even over the other five values.

The logic is simple: good results enable the company to keep doing the right thing. For instance, they are not transparent (another value) for the sake of transparency but because it leads to better outcomes.

Personal needs, even over team preferences

For most remote teams, reconciling personal preferences with team needs is challenging, mainly because many organizations continue to approach collaboration as something that needs to happen synchronously; we'll discuss this in more detail in Step 4.

When GoTo decided to go remote-first, the company created a study to understand the differences across employee groups. The results uncovered five personas: working individually, working with other adults, working with young children, working with school children, and working while caring for adults.

GoTo realized that each group has different needs and expectations. For example, those with school children prefer to book their early morning to be with them and start work later, while people working alone prefer to start earlier and go to the office as much as possible.

The findings drove the company to adopt a flexible approach by prioritizing each group's personal needs, even over what each team needed. People can work on the schedule that best suits their needs.

Well-being, even over productivity

One of my clients, Forma, is a platform that provides benefits designed for the modern workforce. It gives employees the freedom to choose health and wellness options that are right for them rather than dictated by their employer.

It makes sense that Forma prioritizes its own employees' well-being, even over productivity. The fast-growing start-up operates under the principle "We got you covered." When someone gets sick, has a family issue, or needs a break, they don't need to ask for permission or explain what's going on. They just inform the team, and their colleagues reply with, "Take the time that you need and we will take care of your work."

Your culture is defined by what you say yes and no to. Prioritization requires making sacrifices, especially when you have to choose between two good things.

What about you? What are your hybrid team's top three "even over" priorities? Using the examples above as a starting point, consider whether you would adopt those priorities or invert the order. What other tensions are in play that require clarifying which good thing matters the most? It's vital that all team members are aligned on the trade-offs they are willing to make.

Recap

STEP 2: REIMAGINE A SHARED FUTURE

Having a shared future creates alignment among your employees, regardless of where they work from.

A purpose statement expresses how your organization or team serves others and makes an impact on the world.

Clear purpose helps steer your team, especially in times of crisis.

Culture is what you reward and punish—behaviors matter more than words.

Purpose helps define your priorities and clarify decision-making for remote teams.

Now that you're familiar with the benefits of a purpose statement, it's time to craft your own.

YOUR TURN: REIMAGINE YOUR TEAM PURPOSE

A clear team purpose helps align team members with the future they want to create together. It also clarifies why the team exists and how it helps the organization accomplish its larger purpose.

Use the following two-step approach to develop your team's purpose.

First, you'll address three critical questions to help define why your team exists. Next, you'll craft a team purpose statement of your own.

Part 1—Define Why Your Team Exists

#1—What is our job as a team?

In a single sentence, write down what your team does, what it delivers, or what it produces. Have your team members share their ideas; each can contribute two or three. Cluster the responses based on similarities and rank them from most to least important.

If your team delivers or produces several things, try to find one concept that represents the majority of the work. For example, "Our team designs user-friendly online shopping experiences," or, "Our team turns data into valuable insights to improve decision-making across the organization."

#2—Who do we work for?

Identify the different groups or stakeholders your team works for. Choose the top one.

For example, are you helping senior executives across the board make better decisions, or are your insights only for the sales or marketing department? Do you serve a particular office or the entire organization?

#3—What impact do we want to create?

Your team purpose should capture why your team exists. Consider the needs and pain points of who you work for. How can you help them do a better job? Most importantly, what's the end impact you want to create in their lives beyond just a functional contribution?

For example, "Our managers can spend more time leading," or "Advisers can take care of their clients."

The HR department at CVS defines its team purpose as, "To help our leaders hire great talent."

Part 2—Write Your Team Purpose Statement

Use the Mad Lib on the bottom of the Team Purpose Canvas to craft your team purpose statement:

TEAM PURPOSE CANVAS
What drives us to work together   Team: [＿＿＿]   Date: [＿＿＿]

What is our job as a team?	Who do we work for?	What impact do we want to create in the organization and beyond?

Team Purpose Statement Write your team purpose statement using the following Mad Lib

Our Team ＿＿＿＿＿＿＿＿＿＿ to/of ＿＿＿＿＿＿＿＿＿＿
           [how / what we do]   [specific audience]

so that ＿＿＿＿＿＿＿＿＿＿＿
           [intended impact]

Created by Gustavo Razzetti   www.fearlessculture.design
Fearless Culture   Fearless Culture

Use this QR code to download your own free copy of the Team Purpose Canvas.

Here are some examples:

"Our team provides efficient support so that our managers can spend more time leading than performing administrative work."

"Our team continually comes up with new solutions so that our organization stays at the forefront of innovation."

"Our team takes care of our advisers so that they can take care of their clients."

Purpose-driven teams become ambassadors. When employees are part of something bigger than themselves, they inspire others to join the movement.

Your team purpose should complement, not compete with, the organization's. Subcultures are not silos but specific manifestations that feed off each other.

REIGNITE BELONGING

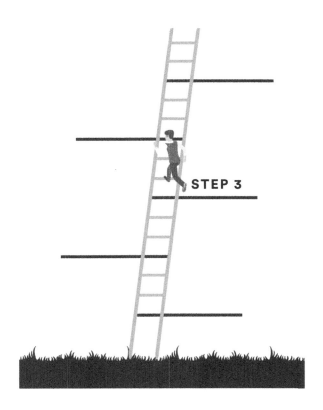

STEP 3

YOU BELONG HERE

Belonging is a fundamental part of being human; we are social animals who need to be connected to others to thrive. Connection makes us feel safe, trusting, and collaborative. It has been in our DNA since ancient times, when being part of a group was literally the difference between life and death.

Leaders tend to underestimate the power of belonging. However, we know that strong personal connections build healthy teams. Strong feelings of belonging is linked to a 56% increase in job performance, better business results, and a healthier workplace culture.[65]

A strong organization is built on a foundation of human connection. People don't just want to be part of a team—they want to *belong*. Creating an environment that honors humanity, not just high performance, is vital for workplace success. This is even more important when employees are working remotely and can't rely on physical proximity to help them bond.

You belong here.

Whakapapa is a Maori idea that embodies our universal human need to belong. It represents a powerful spiritual belief that each person is part of an unbroken and unbreakable chain of people who share a sacred identity and culture.

Over the past decade, Owen Eastwood has become one of the world's most in-demand performance coaches. Elite teams and organizations, from the England football team and the Scotland rugby squad to the Royal Ballet School and the Command Group of NATO, have partnered with him to create a deeper sense of belonging.

Whakapapa is the starting point of Eastwood's work with teams and leaders. It unlocks a sense of identity. This approach works for both established and new teams, extracting meaning from their legacy or shaping a more intentional future, respectively.

In *Belonging: The Ancient Code of Togetherness*, Eastwood wrote: "Each of us are part of an unbreakable chain of people going back and forward in time. Each of us in this chain of people has our arms interlocked with those on either side of us. We are unbreakable. Together, immortal."

When we experience a sense of belonging, our body activates "happy hormones," like serotonin, dopamine, and oxytocin, that promote happiness, pleasure, and even love. This increases trust, connection, and collaboration.

On the other hand, studies have found that social isolation evokes cravings similar to hunger and have located social exclusion in the same region of the brain where we experience physical pain. That's why it's not uncommon for remote teams to feel emotionally as well as physically distanced.

We all share this impulse to be accepted by our tribe. Even introverts need to belong. Harvard professor Amy Edmonson explains this phenomenon in *Fearless Organizations*. "We are almost hardwired to be worried about the impression we make on others." Feeling rejected by our social system feels a lot like dying.

Great teams leverage the power of belonging. Belonging provides shared purpose, values, and norms that shape team behavior. Eastwood says that the ability to form groups is an essential human trait. "You will not be judged by your money or celebrity [status] or sense of self-pride... you will be judged by what you did for our tribe."

Belonging is a feeling that results from being recognized and appreciated by fellow human beings. It makes our life more meaningful. When you are accepted by your team, you don't have to pretend to be someone else.

In Step 3: Belonging, I provide insights and tools you can use to make remote team members feel welcome—to be part of the tribe and how you can use psychological safety, feedback, and rituals to increase belonging.

Am I Connected?

Consciously or not, we are always asking this question.

When you belong, you don't need to be a different person at work. You can speak freely without fearing retribution. You actually enjoy working with your colleagues. Work is not just a job, but an enjoyable experience. Most importantly, a strong sense of belonging increases engagement and reduces turnover by 50%.[66]

Do you feel comfortable being vulnerable with your colleagues? Do you feel safe asking for or offering help? Over time, the interactions make us feel supported and welcomed as human beings.

Author Brené Brown said it best: "A deep sense of love and belonging is an irreducible need of all people. When those needs are not met, we don't function as we were meant to. We break."

Intimacy, vulnerability, and contribution create belonging.

One silver lining of the pandemic was that it helped us appreciate the importance of belonging, especially when working remotely. Traditionally, it was easier for co-located team members to build belonging. Small, in-person interactions, such as having lunch together, chatting over coffee, or attending company events helped people connect with each other. Working remotely put a halt to these practices, causing many remote workers to feel separated from their teams and culture.

Fortunately, belonging doesn't require physical proximity, just a different mindset. You can cultivate a sense of belonging that helps bridge the gap and bring people together despite the distance.

Dr. Tasha Eurich, organizational psychologist and author of *The New York Times* best-selling book *Insight*, recommends leaders to acknowledge the opportunities, not just the challenges. "Virtual meetings offer a surprisingly powerful space for people to contribute and connect. It completely levels the playing field," she told me in an interview. "There's a new way for the more introverted members to contribute: the chat. Offering options in how people contribute and participate creates more inclusive conversations."

The problem is that companies try to replicate the same experience in a virtual setting rather than thinking differently. "Avoid copy-pasting past practices into the new reality," Eurich said. "What are you missing? What did those cultural interactions do for the team? Spell it out." Leaders need to recreate "How did that activity help the teams?" rather than the activity itself.

PSYCHOLOGICAL SAFETY MATTERS NOW MORE THAN EVER

Amy Edmondson defines psychological safety as "the shared belief that the team is safe for interpersonal risk-taking."[67] Psychological safety means that people can bring their full selves to work, speak out, and challenge the status quo without fear of retaliation.

 Simply put, psychological safety is the difference between silence and participation.

Unfortunately, according to Gallup, only 30% of employees strongly agree that their opinions count at work.[68] This is bad news, not just for workers who don't feel comfortable expressing themselves, but for organizations that may not be making the most of their employees' talents.

Safety is not the opposite of risk-taking; it's a conduit to experimentation. A safe environment isn't simply about being "nice" or lowering the bar. Diversity of perspectives, disagreement, and debate are key drivers of innovation.

According to Google research, psychological safety is the secret sauce of high-performing teams.[69] A safe culture makes it easier for quiet voices to speak up, increasing participation of introverts, women, and minority groups—the people who are interrupted or ignored the most.

Psychological safety is similar to but not the same as trust. Trust is built between two people; psychological safety is created by the team. A safe environment isn't dictated top-down by managers; it's built on the contributions of everyone involved.

Working from home has put team culture, and especially psychological safety, to the test for remote teams. Personal life and work overlap now in ways they never did before. Scheduling, staffing, and coordination decisions must take personal issues into account. Building strong relationships has become more challenging, and cues are harder to read when your team is not in the same room.

To address the challenges of remote work, managers and team members must engage in conversations that touch on their identities, values, and personal choices. People now have to work harder to share what they're thinking, to ask questions, or to challenge the status quo. This means we must be more intentional and mindful about creating psychological safety. Creating the right environment allows us to address personal issues without taking them personally.

Edmondson told *Work in Progress*: "Distributed work is making us realize we have to be more deliberately—more proactively—open. We have to be explicit in sharing our ideas, questions, and concerns because we can't just over-hear what's happening in the next cubicle."[70]

A hybrid workplace culture can create a divide between those who are present and those who are working remotely. In Step 1, we discussed the importance of "leveling the playing field"; in other words, creating the same or a similar experience for everyone so that no one feels excluded. Are the "locals" willing to abide by a remote-first practice?

The debate continues over whether working remotely makes it easier or harder for people to participate in meetings or discussions. In my experience, working remotely provides multiple benefits. Minority groups feel safer working from home, and parents say that colleagues are more understanding when family issues get in the way.

Working from home has created "a liberating, more human state of mind," according to Dr. Myriam Hadnes, founder of Never Done Before, the largest global community for facilitators. "You can be working from your couch, in pajamas, enjoying a cup of coffee, feeling free, and still be super productive and creative."

Hadnes believes Zoom calls actually provide a safer space than in-person meetings. As she told me: "In an office, the CEO wouldn't talk to an intern, but breakout rooms have changed that dynamic. With one click, you pair strangers, and they start random conversations. When they're back in the main room, people usually complain that their "private" time wasn't enough. They emerge from the breakout room with a smile."

For most, breakout rooms have become a safe haven. They feel comfortable sharing their emotions, tensions, and issues in a way that wasn't possible in an open office.

CLIMBING THE PSYCHOLOGICAL SAFETY LADDER

Psychological safety is a spectrum; it's not whether you have it, but how much. I use the metaphor of climbing a ladder. Promoting psychological safety requires moving from one rung to the next. We must strive to reach the highest possible level.

However, you can't take progress for granted. You can go up the ladder by increasing psychological safety, but conversely, bad behavior can cause you to drop a few rungs—or even fall off.

The Psychological Safety Ladder includes three levels:

Level 1: Welcome
Level 2: Courageous Conversations
Level 3: Innovation

The graphic below shows the three levels with examples of the kinds of statements we want to be true for each.

Level 1

I feel welcomed by my team

It's easy to ask my colleagues for help

It's okay to talk about health issues and burnout

We know one another personally, not just professionally

Level 2

My unique skills and talents are valued and utilized

I'm not afraid to ask questions and share my thoughts

We can bring up problems and tough issues

My team encourages me to disagree or think differently

Level 3

Questions are always welcome on our team

It's okay to challenge the status quo

We openly share and learn from our mistakes

I feel safe to take risks in this team and experiment

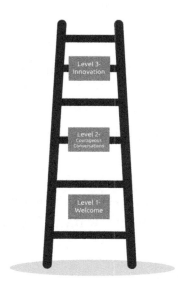

The Three Levels of Psychological Safety

Belonging is a critical element for constructing high-performing teams. It's about feeling safe enough to build strong interpersonal relationships, bring your whole self to work, address well-being issues, and actively participate in meetings or conversations. This is the foundation of Psychological Safety or Level 1.

Level 1: Welcome. Many people confuse "feeling safe" with being risk-averse. That's because they get stuck at Level 1. The purpose of developing an environment of high psychological safety is to promote diverse thinking and innovation. It's an invitation to continue climbing the ladder.

Level 2: Courageous Conversations are critical for teams to perform at their best. This stage is about feeling safe enough to contribute your unique skills and talents, speak up about tough issues, disagree or think differently, and ask for help. Level 2 invites team members to constantly reexamine facts and remain objective. It also encourages greater scrutiny of everyone's actions, improving information processing and decision-making.

Level 3: Innovation addresses the end result of high-performing teams. It's not just about developing new products or services but also about coming up with new solutions that help people work better. Level 3 is about feeling safe in challenging the status quo, using questions to explore what's possible, making mistakes, and experimenting.

As we'll see in the following section, the paradox of psychological safety is that the higher you climb the ladder, the safer you feel taking risks.

BUILDING PSYCHOLOGICAL SAFETY—ONE STEP AT A TIME

So, what's the best way to start climbing the ladder?

In the following pages, I share some activities that you can practice with your team to help you move from one level to the next.

Level 1: Welcome

One year into the pandemic, the strategy team from Saatchi & Saatchi Los Angeles and Dallas had hit rock bottom. Working remotely was taking a toll on people, as it was in most organizations. The strategy team worked with a consultant and discovered that people felt out of touch with colleagues. They were growing disconnected and lacked the sense of belonging they used to have.

The strategy team broke into three groups, one of which focused on psychological safety and self-identifiers. Getting to know people at a different level transforms the rules of engagement, so every week, one person took the stage to talk about themselves. The head of the strategy team went first to model the desired behavior. He shared his story, where he came from, and reflected on his privilege in a transparent way. By modeling vulnerability, the leader made it safe for team members to be vulnerable, too.

Sarah Parsa Nguyen, who spearheaded the psychological safety program at Saatchi & Saatchi, told me: "The key learning is that we can't control what's happening on the outside, but we can control the way we feel about it on the inside. That behavior can shift our behavior toward ourselves and others."

The desire to belong extended to the community, too. Saatchi & Saatchi employees started donating time to local food banks. Nguyen and her team are now prioritizing diverse, local, community-based vendors.

"We are raised to fit in a box, and that's part of the challenge," she said, reflecting on her journey. "It's about going back to the basics of human nature. Back to community, back to our values, back to yourselves. Be kind to your neighbor."

True belonging is about reconnecting with ourselves and our colleagues. Carve out time to slack off a little. Get to know your colleagues better and let them know that you value them beyond the work they do. The following exercises can help.

What's your superpower? What's your kryptonite?

A team is the sum of multiple skills, perspectives, and abilities. The purpose of this exercise is to get to know your colleagues better. More importantly, it's about how you complement each other's strengths and weaknesses.

Invite each team member to reflect on their superpower (their unique strength) and kryptonite (what drains their energy or makes them powerless). Ask people to choose one superpower and one kryptonite to share.

Debrief on commonalities and differences—how can they complement each other?

Encourage people to move beyond "good" and "bad." It's how we use our abilities that really matter. For example, my superpower is to connect and make sense of things that seem unrelated, and my kryptonite is getting frustrated. However, I've learned to turn frustration into action. Rather than getting stuck because things didn't go my way, I act on the things I *can* control. Conversely, if I'm always trying to find connections, it can be exhausting.

Check-in rounds

Starting meetings with time for personal sharing has become more common since working from home became the norm. Check-in rounds help us empathize with our team members, understand what's really going on, and avoid judging them.

An assigned facilitator invites people to share one at a time; each participant should pay attention without interrupting or reacting to the person who's sharing.

One interesting question is, "What's got your attention?" This prompts sharing worries, preoccupations, or distractions.

Here are some additional questions you can use:

- What kind of a day have you had so far today?
- What words would you use to describe where your head is? And where your heart is?
- Share a one- or two-word intention you hold for today's meeting/conversation.

Metaphors work well too, especially for those who don't like to talk about emotions. The weather is a perfect conduit. Ask participants, "What was the weather like for your work this past week?"

Check-In Round

What was the weather like for your work this past week?

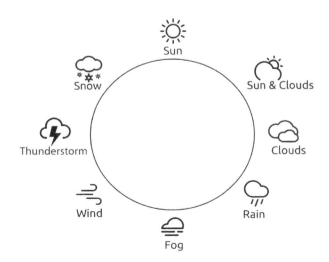

When people can check-in their emotions, they no longer feel the pressure to bottle them up and can relax, knowing that they are still accepted by the team.

36 questions that turn strangers into friends

Empathy is crucial to building trust. The more we get to know and understand our colleagues, the more we can trust each other. Stories are the perfect way to increase a sense of belonging and start building psychological safety among teams.

The purpose of this exercise is to get to know your colleagues on a deeper level. That's the power of stories. Interesting questions open dialogue and multiple possibilities. That's what Arthur Aron discovered with his list of 36 questions.

Divide your team into pairs and have them use these questions to get started (you can find the full list of 36 questions at bit.ly/the36questions:

1. Given the choice of anyone in the world, whom would you want as a dinner guest?
2. Would you like to be famous? In what way?
3. What would constitute a "perfect" day for you?
4. When did you last sing to yourself? To someone else?
5. If a crystal ball could tell you the truth, what would you want to know about your future?
6. What is the greatest accomplishment of your life?
7. What do you value most in a friendship?

8. When did you last cry?
9. Share an embarrassing moment in your life.

The more we know our colleagues on a personal level, the better we perform. Encourage your team to have more personal conversations and share meaningful stories.

Washing instructions

Break the Golden Rule: don't treat people how *you* want to be treated; instead, follow their "washing instructions."

This activity, created by Agile coach Pia-Maria Thorén, uses laundry labels as a metaphor to help team members describe how they want to be treated. As she points out, some people, like some clothes, may need to be treated delicately or washed separately. Others may object to having their ideas ironed out or may shrink in hot water.

Invite team members to create theirs and have them share one at a time.

Some examples to inspire your team:

- Don't talk to me before I've had my morning coffee
- Give me feedback often—both good and bad
- Don't ask me personal things in front of others
- Ideas are always welcome; no need to ask for permission to challenge me
- Don't just share the *what*, explain the *why*

- I like to think before speaking; it gives me time to reflect before I respond
- I'm good at the big picture; don't ask me to take care of details
- I do my best work when I have freedom; don't micro-manage me
- I love loud music

The 5-Second Rule

Silence usually signals that people don't feel safe to share what they're thinking. However, silence is also necessary for understanding. If everyone's talking, who's paying attention?

We know silence is uncomfortable. However, not paying attention or interrupting each other is much worse. The 5-Second Rule is a technique to encourage people to become better at listening and provides a space for people to reflect, to speak up.

If you're facilitating a meeting, pause after you ask a question. Don't surrender to the pressure to fill the silence with more noise. Slowly count up to five. Those five seconds will feel like an eternity for you and the team.

If silence feels uncomfortable in person, imagine how most people feel when they have to speak out in a group video call. The 5-Second Rule is a pause that invites people to enter the conversation. For example, when you ask, "Any questions?" wait silently for at least five seconds before speaking again.

Walk in your colleagues' shoes

Perspective-taking is the perfect exercise to mentally walk in someone else's shoes. It develops empathy by inviting team members to reflect on the challenges minority groups face and becoming more supportive and understanding.

Guide the team through this activity following these steps:

1. Have all team members share their backgrounds considering multiple characteristics (education, sexual orientation, race, religion, etc.)—capture all responses to codify the diverse profile of the team
2. Pair each team member with someone whose background is completely different from their own across one or many variables
3. Have each person write a few lines on the unique challenges they imagine their partner has to deal with because of their background
4. Encourage each duo to share and discuss findings
5. Debrief with the entire team

Perspective-taking produces more empathic teams, according to research. It helps build positive attitudes and behaviors toward minorities.

Use your camera intentionally

There's a lot of debate about whether participants should keep their cameras on or off during online meetings. What people miss is that it's not a binary issue—it all depends on the context.

We know that nonverbal cues are important. That's why many people consider "camera on" as the polite thing to do. Others feel it invades their privacy. Managers may wonder whether participants who have their cameras off are engaged or are multitasking.

Most importantly, the camera challenges unconscious behavior. As Tasha Eurich explains, "Remote requires us to override tens of hundreds of thousand years of hardwired wired human behaviors. We like to make eye contact. It's easy in person, we do it both at the same time. In Zoom, if you want to show that you are making eye contact, you have to look away from the person and into the camera."

Eurich believes that leaders and organizations should think more strategically and intentionally about how they use technology. Defaulting to video meetings could be extremely draining over time. Even Zoom (the company) has Zoom-free days. Eurich likes to encourage leaders to give video a break and see what happens. "Hey, guys, we are not going to turn on our cameras today. We are just going to listen."

Align your team with a common flexibility approach. A lack of reciprocation can hurt people's feelings. Use the following criteria as a starting point:

Turn your camera ON if:

- You are leading the meeting or presenting
- You want to show that you are present
- You are brainstorming or doing group activities
- You are meeting people for the first time
- You are in a small group or breakout room
- You are discussing sensitive topics

Turn your camera OFF if:

- You're not playing an active role in the meeting
- The meeting doesn't require much interaction
- The meeting has a large number of participants
- There's a lot going on in the room you're in
- You simply need a break from the camera
- During breaks

Level 2: Courageous Conversations

When the pandemic started, Volvo's leadership naturally wanted to put all leadership training on hold. Like most organizations, they wanted to focus on the short-term crisis and postpone training until things got back to normal. However, the leadership development team pushed back—they didn't want to cancel training.

"We are going to go online to help leaders, who we know are scared, lost, and need support," Volvo's Global Head of Leadership and Culture Liz Rider shared when I interviewed her.

It's rare that people feel safe enough in their organization to think differently or push back. Not only that, but Volvo's leadership development team was able to embrace intellectual humility and vulnerability, admitting that "it doesn't have to be perfect." The team took its chances despite a lack of experience managing online training on a large scale.

The first session of the program was about feedback. Participants were invited to hold self-managed conversations in breakout rooms. Rider remembers: "It was a revolt. People didn't want to do it alone; they expected me to facilitate the conversations. However, once they came back to the main room, everyone was excited."

Going virtual transformed Volvo's approach to leadership development. Volvo now offers a digital learning journey with shorter, more digestible modules that equip leaders with new insights and tools faster. In just over one year, 2,000 leaders have gone through the training, creating a stronger community, as leaders from multiple regions interacted and learned together.

Psychological safety is crucial for organizations to improve. People need to feel safe to speak up and share their ideas, and even to push back against leaders. The following exercises/ principles will help you promote courageous conversations.

Design participation to include everyone

One of the benefits of having a psychologically safe team is being able to tap into the collective wisdom, but it takes proper facilitation to ensure everyone speaks up. Amy Edmondson once told me to ask "What might at least one person be thinking and reluctant to say aloud?"

Conversations are your team's currency, and their value depends on participation.

Australian tech unicorn Atlassian practices conversational turn-taking to ensure equal participation. Every person is given their turn to speak and the rest must listen. The facilitators invite quiet people to go first. Leaders and louder people always speak last so they don't influence or intimidate others.

Protect introverts from extroverts

The goal of this activity is for people to become more aware of their colleagues' participation styles as well as their own, so that they can adjust behaviors and improve participation.

Ask people to reflect on their participation style. Do they think to talk, or talk to think? Do they consider themselves shy or outspoken?

Once everyone has mapped themselves, let them share their participation style with others. Then have the team reflect to discuss the differences and how to become more aware of their colleagues' styles.

Last, discuss how everyone can adjust their behaviors to improve participation. Some may learn to take space, others to make space.

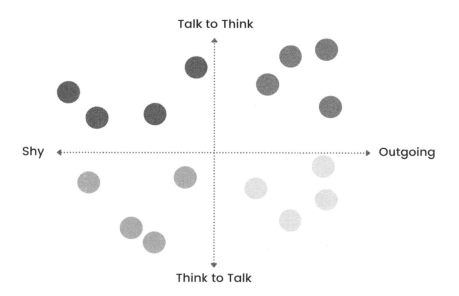

No-interruptions rule

What's the point of inviting someone to a meeting only to have another silence them? Constant interruptions turn meetings into a painful experience, increasing anxiety and silence.

The "no-interruptions rule" is simple: when someone is talking, everyone else should actively listen. Interrupt the interrupter. Protect the room so people feel safe to speak freely.

Be polite but firm. Atlassian's former Global Head of Diversity & Belonging Aubrey Blanche suggests using a phrase such as, "Hold on, Bob. I want to make sure I understand Jessica's point before moving on."

The no-interruptions rule improves the quality of conversations. Protect all voices and deal privately with repeat interrupters.

Nothing about me without me

This guiding principle ensures that people are consulted during decision-making, especially those affected by a decision.

If a decision will affect people's jobs, future, personal lives, etc., it makes total sense to include them in the process. It doesn't mean that the final decision will keep everyone happy, but it does ensure that every voice is heard and considered.

The Advice Process, a term coined by Dennis Bakke, former CEO of AES Corporation, states that before making a decision, you must first seek input from

- Everyone who will be significantly affected by the decision
- People with expertise in the topic at hand

Seeking input doesn't mean achieving consensus. It's a commitment to ensure people's interests will be considered and weighed before a decision is made.

Silence = disagreement

We were trained to assume that silence gives consent. However, that's not usually the case.

The truth is, people have a hard time expressing disagreement. Leaders should reframe the meaning of silence to confirm whether or not there's alignment. In *The Advantage*, Patrick Lencioni recommends changing the meaning of silence to "no." Rather than assuming that people agree when they stay silent, infer that they don't.

Before closing an action item in a meeting, ask for feedback: "Does everyone agree?" Assume that silence means no. Before moving to the next item on the agenda, encourage everyone to verbally confirm they're on board.

Uncover the stinky fish

The issues that your team avoids won't magically go away. In fact, they'll get worse over time. "Stinky fish" is a metaphor for issues that we don't want to talk about. The longer we avoid a problem, the stinker it gets, and it will end up contaminating everything around us.

Have your team capture issues using the following four questions:

- What are your uncertainties?
- What makes you feel anxious or nervous?

- What is everybody thinking but no one is saying?
- What are past issues we can't get over?

After everyone has had a chance to write down answers on sticky notes, ask members to share one at a time. Facilitate a couple of rounds to help people gradually open up. Focus on creating clusters and then prioritizing the top three issues that you want to tackle first.

This activity requires several rounds. Don't worry if people can't move past trivial issues the first time. Get them talking and becoming more comfortable with addressing issues in the open.

People love getting their stinky fish out of the system. With practice, it sparks courageous conversations.

UNCOVER THE STINKY FISH

Speaking up is the first step to solve silent problems

Team name [   ]   Date [   ]

What are your uncertainties?

What's making you feel afraid or anxious?

What is everybody thinking and no one is saying?

What are the past issues we can't get over?

Created by Gustavo Razzetti
FearlessCulture - V 1.1

www.fearlessculture.design

Fearless Culture

Use the following QR code to download your free copy.

Celebrate the messenger

It's easy to speak out when you have good news to share. But what happens when you have to bring bad news to your manager or team?

Amy Edmondson encourages leaders to embrace the messenger. Don't accuse people of being the problem. Rather than attacking the bearer of bad news, focus on the data; if you know something is not working, you can fix it. OpenTable's former CEO Christa Quarles said, "No amount of ugly truth scares me. It's just information to make a decision."

Look for ways to encourage people to raise difficult topics and reward them when they do. Help people reframe "bad news" as data. Celebrate the messenger instead of vilifying those who bring issues forward. Respect those who speak up. Don't kill the messenger because you don't like the news; be thankful that they are giving you valuable information.

Level 3: Innovation

Steve Jobs almost prevented Apple from creating the most profitable product in the world. His team was trying to convince him that a cell phone was a perfect fit for Apple, but Jobs hated mobile phones and cell phone companies. The notion of developing an Apple phone was "the dumbest idea I've ever heard."

Luckily, Apple's culture, a culture of innovation where people are committed to doing their best—and fighting for their ideas—saved the company from its founder's reluctance.

After months of discussion, Jobs gave his blessing and two teams were tasked with experimenting with different paths. Should Apple add calling capabilities to the iPod or turn the Mac into a tiny tablet that doubled as a phone? As a result, the first iPhone was born. The rest is history.

Even though Jobs was a visionary leader, without his team's perseverance and pushback, the iPhone wouldn't exist today. A psychologically safe culture helped protect what it's now Apple's most successful product.

The following techniques and exercises can help you create an environment in which people feel safe enough to bring their full creativity to the table.

Increase your tolerance for mistakes

Organizations often ask people to take risks and experiment more. However, most employees are afraid of making mistakes because they fear retaliation.

Do you encourage people to celebrate errors or to bury them? Does your team feel supported or is it afraid of being punished? Do you focus on finding the lesson or on finding the scapegoat?

Tolerating mistakes doesn't mean lowering the bar. It means understanding that mistakes are stepping stones, not disasters. Face mistakes with a learning mindset, not a blaming one.

At social media company NixonMcInnes, people confess their mistakes at Church of Fail and are wildly applauded for doing so. Making failure socially acceptable has contributed to an open and creative culture.

1-2-4-All

Brainstorming sessions or large meetings can be intimidating. People feel more comfortable talking to strangers than those they'll see again, or to one single person than to a larger group. Most of us don't feel psychologically safe speaking up and sharing our ideas openly.

The 1-2-4-All method is one of the 30 Liberating Structures, a compilation of microstructures for facilitating meetings and conversations developed by Keith McCandless and Henri Lipmanowicz.

This method is ideal for encouraging progressive participation in problem-solving sessions. People start brainstorming on their own, then in duos, then in teams of four, and finally, all together. It promotes creativity by allowing people to share their ideas gradually.

Follow this sequence: Allow people to work on their own. Then, pair people up and give each duo two minutes to share individual ideas. Next, give them two to three minutes to discuss and find surprises, contradictions, and commonalities. They should also use this time to build on each other's ideas. Finally, pair up the twosomes into sets of four. Rinse and repeat until the entire group has worked together.

You can also use the 1-2-4-All for addressing courageous conversations, for example, to debrief the stinky fish activity.

Silent brainstorming

Silent brainstorming (or silent storming) is an alternative way to get people to come up with ideas. It allows participants to think without distraction or be influenced by others.

It took me a while to embrace this technique. My approach to brainstorming has been deeply influenced by my time at Stanford's business school. Many years later, I've come to realize that having a group of people brainstorming out loud, frenetically, and all at the same time, is not very effective for introverts. This is especially true in a remote environment.

A silent brainstorm allows participants to come up with new ideas in silence, at their own pace, and without external influence. It helps overcome groupthink and peer pressure. Many studies show that silent brainstorming generates better creative ideas.[71]

Share a challenge and allow people to contribute with their ideas. Ideally, you don't want others to see who's writing what. Then have people share their best ideas out loud and everyone can build from each other's ideas with a "yes, and…" approach.

Consolidate and cluster ideas.

A well-facilitated remote brainstorming can get better results than in-person sessions.

Eliminate the clutter

One of the biggest challenges of brainstorming is selecting good ideas. When people vote on ideas, they usually reward mediocre ones. This is even more noticeable when voting remotely—they play it safer.

Too many ideas are daunting and can cloud our judgment. It's important for the team to take a break after a brainstorming session. Distance provides perspective and allows people to choose the right ideas without the pressure of time.

I've been using the following approach with remote teams with excellent results: Before voting on ideas, encourage your team to eliminate any that are a distraction. Start by removing ideas that offer nothing new, are too conservative, or don't necessarily solve the problem at hand. Rather than "idea selection," practice "noise elimination."

Now challenge the remaining ideas, one by one. Is this a concept that we feel proud of? Will this idea take us to the next level? How will I feel tomorrow if this is the only idea that gets approved? Use similar questions to complete a second elimination round.

Eliminating the noise makes it safe for people to protect the best ideas.

Keep it small

Remote meetings are full of challenges. These problems only amplify as meeting size increases, when airtime becomes scarce and people quickly disengage from the conversation.

The number one rule in team performance is: as the size of a team increases, productivity and creativity decrease. For more productive discussions or brainstorming sessions, team up in smaller groups of, ideally, five to seven people.

Dividing larger groups into smaller, virtual breakouts provides the benefit of parallel processing. Each group can see the problem from a different angle or find alternative solutions. Encourage the other teams to push back and find the flaws.

Encourage unreasonable solutions

The best ideas often get killed before they see the light of day because they are deemed "unreasonable." We judge them too early in the game, before we can see their true potential.

Sometimes, it pays to think impractically. That's the case of Corning, one of the world's leading innovators in material science. CEO Wendell Weeks has built a reputation for encouraging unreasonable solutions. When one engineer proposed a solution for increasing the efficiency of a technology by 25%, Weeks asked, "Why not 50%?" This "unreasonable" challenge helped uncover new possibilities that would have been otherwise overlooked.

Use prompts to encourage people to come up with unreasonable ideas. I use one that people love: "Ideas that could get you fired." The prompt gives people permission to come up with wild ideas.

The voice of the employee

Raising issues individually is hard; it's easier to speak truth to power when a neutral ambassador can represent team members' interests. It not only depersonalizes the conversation but turns it into a two-way street.

Zappos practices using the voice of employees (VOE), a biweekly meeting to uncover and address tensions across the organization.[72]

VOE is an open space where randomly selected representatives from different departments get together to "bubble up and bubble down" concerns, feedback, and ideas. The group discusses issues with the leaders of the company and then reports back.

This approach has helped Zappos's leadership become more aware of untapped issues affecting both customers and employees and has sparked collective innovation.

FEEDBACK IS A GIFT (NOT A PUNISHMENT)

For years, managers have been taught to praise or criticize just about everything their employees do.

Most people resist feedback because it makes them feel attacked. Just the thought of feedback triggers negative reactions that make our hearts pound, precipitating worry and anxiety. And no wonder. Feedback has become a corrective action, a tool to fix people—and most people don't enjoy feeling like they need to be "fixed."

It's no surprise, then, that employees hate performance reviews. According to a study by Francesca Gino, professor of business administration at Harvard Business School, 89% of people do not look forward to their reviews.[73]

When Keith Bailey took the reins of one of Transpacific Industries' most troubled divisions, it wasn't the business model that was the problem so much as the stories the company told itself.[74] Deceptive organizational messages reflected both bygone glories ("We're extraordinary. Rules don't apply to us.") and skepticism about the future ("No one can save this company. There's going to be a bloodbath.").

Neither of those narratives were accurate. However, Bailey had to reframe the conversation to turn around the crumbling organization. He had to address issues in the open.

Most companies suffer from deceptive organizational messages that promote a self-defeating mindset. Usually, these conversations happen behind closed doors and can be hard to root out.

There are three types of stories that create cognitive distortions:

- Victim stories ("It's not my fault")
- Villain stories ("It's the leader's fault")
- Helpless stories ("There's nothing I can do")

Feedback uncovers the way things really are. The first step is recognizing deceptive messages for what they are and reframing the narrative. Bailey spent two years facilitating open conversations with the leadership team, using feedback to surface issues and exploring new possibilities.

This CEO turned feedback into an inquiry. Rather than reacting by telling people they were wrong, Bailey asked, "How did this narrative become part of our culture?" Rather than having individual sessions, he tackled feedback collectively and in the open. Executives were skeptical when he asked for input, but finally came around.

In one pivotal session, Bailey brought together all the functional leaders and managers in the organization. He asked participants to prepare to share their expectations for the future. After everyone shared their feedback, the CEO shared his own notes. To everyone's surprise, they were more aligned than anticipated. Within five hours, the team uncovered 130 problems and identified the seven they wanted to solve first.

Bailey was able to reframe the self-defeating narrative by shifting the focus. Feedback became a tool to uncover possibilities rather than rehash past issues and negative perceptions. Transpacific Industries was able to recover, even winning the Turnaround of the Year award.[75]

Bailey turned feedback into a gift that people wanted to receive.

The Feedback Fallacy

The research is clear: telling others what they should improve actually *hinders* learning.

In a revealing Harvard Business Review article, Marcus Buckingham and Ashley Goodall describe the feedback fallacy—why feedback rarely achieves what it's supposed to.[76] Current feedback practices are based on three theories that most managers accept as truth. However, the authors pointed out those concepts are *wrong*.

The **theory of the source of truth** posits that others know your weaknesses better than you do.

The **theory of learning** presumes that your colleagues should teach you the abilities you lack.

The **theory of excellence** assumes that performance is universal and describable and that it can be transferred from managers to employees.

These three theories have one thing in common: they are based on the assumption that managers have the ability to fix everyone's flaws.

Citing multiple studies, Buckingham and Goodall debunked all three. The most significant insight is the realization that we are not reliable judges of others. Research shows that more than 50% of our assessment of someone else reflects our perception of their abilities, rather than the abilities themselves. For instance, men tend to give female employees softened, less candid feedback because they perceive women as less confident.[77] This hinders female employees' self-assessment and improvement.

Feedback: Focus on the System, Not the Individual

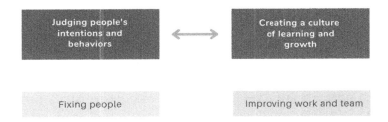

 Criticism creates a fight-or-flight response, so rehashing our flaws tends to inhibit rather than enable learning. Most of the time, we simply shut down. Feedback fails when it's practiced from a place of fear, judgment, and separation.

Stop trying to fix people. Create a culture of learning and growth instead. The following five shifts can help you turn feedback into a gift that everyone wants to receive—and give.

5 Shifts for Better Feedback

Shift #1: From annual performance reviews to casual, regular feedback

Performance reviews are slow, expensive, and time-consuming. Even worse, research shows that they don't improve behavior. On the contrary, they make people feel intimidated, promoting toxic behaviors such as individualism and lack of collaboration.

Microsoft's historically toxic culture was the result of a broken performance review method based on a stack ranking. "Stack ranking" slots employees into "high-performing" and "low-performing" percentiles, sometimes with the threat that the lowest-ranked employees will be fired. Not surprisingly, this method promoted individualism and internal competition. People cared more about surviving than doing the right thing.[78]

Microsoft not only got rid of stack ranking, but even banned the word "feedback" because the connotations were so negative. Instead, the tech company implemented a more personal, friendly approach. "Perspectives" is a system that encourages employees to praise as well as critique each other. It makes conversations less intimidating, prompting dialogue that feels more like coaching than a review. People are open to receiving feedback but have the option of whether to use the gift or not.

Shift #2: From giving to requesting feedback

Most managers were trained to give feedback, not to receive it. They operate as the source of truth, often judging employees. Not only do they fail to change people's behavior, but they don't always do a great job of learning themselves.

Patagonia eliminated performance ratings and implemented a system of continuous feedback and quarterly check-ins. However, the most significant change was encouraging managers to be receivers, not just givers. The outdoor clothing and gear company realized that wise leaders receive more feedback than they give. They focus on what they can improve rather than on what others should do.

Patagonia's CHRO Dean Carter explained, "When you ask for feedback, you create generosity in the system and it explodes exponentially. It's much more powerful to ask than to just get it unsolicited."

Patagonia has created a culture of collective feedback by training managers to ask for feedback rather than provide it. By modeling being a good receiver, they're encouraging others to ask for the gift of feedback, too.

Shift #3: From top-down to peer-to-peer feedback

As companies adapt to new ways of working, top-down feedback practices are losing relevance. As more teams adopt agile and self-organizing models, the role of the manager is becoming less important in reviewing people's performance.[79]

Not only can your colleagues provide a more accurate picture of your work than your boss, but peer feedback boosts employee performance, according to technology research and consulting company Gartner.[80]

At Fitzii, the recruitment software company, employees greatly appreciate the self- and peer-review process.[81] Every year, each employee completes a self-assessment, focusing on two things:

- The past year's performance: accomplishments, learning, and mistakes
- The specific areas in which they'd like to get feedback

Self-assessments are then shared with all Fitzii team members, who review the content before responding to

- What their colleagues did well, the one thing they value most about working with them
- What feedback they want to give that could best help their colleague grow or improve (in the areas that the colleague is interested in hearing about)

Feedback *is not* an objective truth, but a perspective. Peers are encouraged to write in "I" language. No numerical ratings or rankings are used. Peer feedback captures how employees have been inspired, touched, or hurt by their colleagues.

Shift #4: From closed and individual to open and collective

Collective feedback helps improve both the team and work, replacing blame with accountability. Rather than a tool to tell people what you think about their performance, feedback should help build a culture of learning and growth. A culture of open, transparent feedback creates ownership. It shifts the conversation from "How can I play better?" to "How can we improve as a team?"

That's exactly the feedback approach of the All Blacks. Individually, all the members of the New Zealand national rugby team review videos of previous games and training sessions. Then, everyone comes together for a collective feedback session. The players review their own performances, holding each other accountable with facts or data. There are no hard feelings. Feedback is about what's best for the team.

The team recognizes that there's no progress without learning and growth; the rugby team learns from every training session and match, whether they win or not.

Shift #5: From rehashing past issues to designing the future

Feedback tends to rehash past issues, which is why most people resist it. Instead of helping us learn from our mistakes, feedback becomes a constant reminder of our errors, making us feel unworthy.

What if we could use feedback to jump into the future rather than being stuck in the past? Or, borrowing from executive coach Marshall Goldsmith, let's replace feed*back* with feed*forward*.

That's exactly what Spotify does, says global HR partner Johan Sellgren. "We try to hold individual 'development talks' where we address the future, the now, and the past."[82] The digital music service organization applies the 70/20/10 formula. Feedback conversations should spend only 10% on the past, 20% on the present, and 70% on the future. It's not that Spotify doesn't believe in learning from the past; the company prefers to relentlessly focus on the present and future.

At Spotify, feedback addresses development, not judgment:

- Where are we and where do we want to go?
- What do we need to do or improve to get there?

Build a Culture of Feedback: 5 Shifts

01	FREQUENT	From annual performance reviews to casual, regular feedback.
02	REQUESTED	From giving to requesting feedback.
03	DEMOCRATIC	From top-down to peer-to-peer feedback.
04	COLLECTIVE	From closed and individual to open and collective.
05	FEEDFORWARD	From rehashing past issues to designing the future.

GIVING FEEDBACK REMOTELY IS HARD—BUT IT DOESN'T HAVE TO BE *THAT* HARD

In my research, I've discovered that feedback has suffered in a hybrid workplace. Faced with connection glitches, the inability to read body language, and the awkwardness of talking to a camera, managers I've interviewed have told me they'd prefer to wait until they can give feedback in person.

However, giving feedback remotely doesn't have to be that hard, it just requires thinking differently.[83] But also, let's not forget that giving feedback in person was uncomfortable, too.

As Ivan Houston, technical capabilities manager at Liberty IT, told me: "The upside is that when you are having a confidential conversation, it is more private remotely. Whereas at the office, when people saw someone meeting with me, in my office behind closed doors, they immediately assumed something wrong was going on."

After almost two years in a hybrid setting, the executive and his team have become more comfortable addressing feedback remotely, even for tough issues.

Giving feedback in a hybrid environment is not only necessary but can be very effective. Below are some principles to help you get you started.

1. Assume Positive Intent

Always operate from the idea that a person meant well or gave their best, no matter what they said or did. It will save you a lot of headaches. Feedback won't work for either the giver or receiver without a basic foundation of trust.

William Singleton of Mars Wrigley expanded on this when he told me: "I assume confusion over conspiracies. I don't believe anyone wakes up thinking how to make things complicated. Especially for new employees who are trying to figure things out."

We naturally have a double standard when it comes to the actions of others. We blame circumstances for our own mistakes, but individuals for theirs. Social psychologists call this bias the Fundamental Attribution Error.[84] It's the tendency to believe that what people do reflects who they are—we attribute errors to character or personality.

Before judging people, assume positive intent. Look at the behavior the person is displaying and stay neutral about its intention. Ask questions. Focus on understanding the situational factors behind behavior rather than judging the person.

2. Manage Conflict in the Open

In a remote environment, signals are hard to read. You have to pay special attention and sense how team members are doing. Most importantly, you want to address minor issues before they become a conflict.

One of GitLab's core values is (radical) transparency; it helps improve relationships, operations, and the business. As GitLab Senior All-Remote Campaign Manager Jessica Reeder told me: "How we manage conflict is embedded in a nonjudgmental culture. Our values are idealistic, yet rooted in concrete outcomes. Disagreement is okay; not getting along is welcomed. But you must address conflict constructively."

Everything at GitLab is public by default, including conflict. Employees are encouraged to be direct and transparent with each other. "We try to channel our inner Ben Horowitz by being both straightforward and kind."[85] Feedback is always about the work and not personal. That doesn't mean it is an easy conversation. However, addressing issues is better than letting them fester.

Most remote-first companies are adopting the idea of managing conflict in the open. Employees are expected to share feedback with others, respectfully disagree, and commit to finding solutions together. At Slack, leaders model openness; they encourage addressing issues in public channels.

Tasha Eurich believes that the way you manage conflict remotely depends on your company culture.[86] Some organizations are ready to practice radical candor; others need support to get there.

Codify your approach to conflict—what should be addressed in the open, and what should not be. Sharing positive feedback should be practiced in the open. This helps team members feel that their work is valued reinforces positive behavior. However, more sensitive topics require one-to-one conversations.

As Reeder explained, "Work-related, ideas, tactical issues are managed directly, openly, and right away. More sensitive topics—ideological, personal, or huge strategic differences—are managed in private."

Leaders tend to struggle with difficult conversations in any environment, virtual or not. But many have found it easier to deal with conflict contained to a computer in the safety of their home. Some people might prefer a video call, others may prefer doing it over the phone.

The most important thing is to set up clear rules of engagement.

3. Take a Break

When we stop trying to respond immediately, we can process and respond more thoughtfully.

Apply the 5-Second Rule I shared previously. Resist the need to fill the void so you can make space for others to reflect and talk in their own time.

If you're having a feedback session, pause after asking a question. Don't surrender to the pressure to fill the silence. Slowly count to five. Let people reflect before they answer.

Creating a pause allows closing one conversation item before moving to the next. This helps both givers and receiver process what's going on. As Hundred's Head of Culture Sarah LC Smith said, "The real key—practice, practice, practice. 'Thank you for the feedback,' pause, breathe, process. 'Can you share more?' Pause, breathe, and process. 'How can we work together to improve this?'"

Sometimes, you might need to take an actual break to avoid things getting out of control.

Carin Taylor, the chief diversity officer for Workday reflected on a conflict with a colleague over a series of virtual conversations.[87] "One of the things that became really important was to give each other a pause and adjust process, think about what was going on." Taking a break helped Taylor feel refreshed, providing both colleagues with a fresh start.

Taking a break turns giving and receiving feedback into a calmer experience.

4. Just Listen

Feedback comes in many shapes and forms. Sometimes, the best help you can offer is your silence. Don't rush to provide a solution. Just listen.

People can learn more from their own experience than from your advice. Processing past events helps us reflect on what we can do better next time.

Have a no-advice feedback meeting. Invite your colleague to talk about a recent issue. Ask them, "How are you today?" and let them talk freely. Just be there, listen, and make space to discuss their fears and feelings.

For follow-up questions, you can ask, "What worked? What didn't work? and Why?" Most importantly, "What will you do differently next time?"

Don't assume that feedback always requires providing a solution. Sometimes, people just want to be listened to. Create a space for reflection, not advice. Let your team find the solution.

Agile coach Cesar Mori Fuentes recommends thoughtful listening: "Focus on the problem and not on the person. Use powerful questions so people evaluate themselves and can identify what they need to improve. If you want to be heard, the first thing you have to do is listen."

5. Establish a Buddy System

Accountability partnerships or success duos help build strong interpersonal relationships and strengthen culture. A team is as strong as the sum of all those relationships.

Multiple organizations, including Buffer, Microsoft, and GitLab, use onboarding buddies to provide a better experience for new hires. However, the benefits of having a buddy shouldn't end there. At Liberty IT, the buddy system goes beyond welcoming new employees and helping them set up their equipment—they become the new hire's go-to person. Partnerships are designed, matching two people that will make sense for both.

"Many people don't have experience coaching others, so we train them. We help them feel comfortable, clarify expectations for buddies, and support them throughout the process," Houston told me. "There are no stupid questions. But if you have a stupid question, come to me."

A buddy becomes the go-to person beyond understanding how things work and the company culture. It becomes a trusting relationship in which to get help and support—from advice or coaching to someone who can listen or hold them accountable.

6. Set Regular One-on-Ones

Having regular conversations to see how people are doing, discuss progress, and address barriers is critical for remote team members. Not only should managers hold regular one-on-ones, but team members should have them with each other, too.

One-on-ones should focus *less* on tracking progress or monitoring people and *more* on ensuring people are okay and set up for success.

Open-ended questions spark a two-way conversation. Follow the flow, not your questionnaire. Here are some examples:

- How's life outside of work?
- What's one thing you're excited about? What's one thing you're worried about?
- What obstacles are getting in your way? How can I help?
- Share a recent win and a recent mistake. What have you learned from both?
- Who's doing a great job and why?
- Am I providing enough clarity and direction?
- Where would you like me more involved? Where would you like me less involved?
- How do you find working with your colleagues? What can we do to improve our team culture?

Establish a regular cadence for one-on-ones and protect that time. Rescheduling this type of conversation because of urgent issues sends the wrong message.

Make one-on-ones optional, too. If a person doesn't want to meet one week, it's okay to opt out. However, if they cancel two or three times in a row, it could be a sign that something's wrong. Once again, assume positive intent and find out.

7. Integrate Asynchronous and Synchronous Feedback

Research shows that casual, unplanned communication dramatically reduces conflict when you're not in the same location.[88] Regular, small doses of feedback can help tackle issues before they escalate. That's why integrating both synchronous and asynchronous feedback practices is vital.

Synchronous feedback happens live, in real-time. It's the most traditional format. When companies were forced to work remotely, they started using virtual tools but continue to practice feedback in real-time.

Asynchronous feedback provides more opportunities for team members to improve behavior without having to get together. Everyone can experience it on their own time and also encourages people to practice it more often.

Synchronous feedback is better for bonding, personal issues, and sensitive conversations (e.g., discussing performance issues, career path/promotion, etc.).

Asynchronous works well for simple, less sensitive topics, but also elicits more thoughtful responses.

For example, when presenting a design or new proposal (synchronously), everyone feels the need to jump in and provided their impressions right away. Asynchronous feedback, on the other hand, provides time to think individually, more specifically, and avoid groupthink.[89] It encourages people to be more thoughtful and intentional.

Discuss the benefits of both asynchronous and synchronous feedback with your team and establish clear rules on how to use each.

BUILD A CULTURE OF COLLECTIVE FEEDBACK

A culture of collective feedback focuses on the system rather than the individual. It encourages people to concentrate on creating a shared outcome, not on figuring out whom to blame. If you want people to collaborate, to act as a team, shouldn't they practice feedback as one?

Giving feedback in a team setting doesn't necessarily mean getting rid of one-on-one conversations. However, in my experience coaching high-performing teams, the number of problems that need to be discussed in a private setting tends to decrease once people get used to addressing issues as a group.

 Collective feedback replaces blame with shared accountability. Rather than fixing people, focus on the system. Experiment with the following exercises to create a culture of collective feedback.

Shared Gifting

Make sure everyone's uses gallery view so they can see each other. On the screen, share a circle with everyone's names and choose who will start. The first person has to provide feedback to the individual to the left of them on the circle. Then the person who was receiving feedback (the receiver) becomes the giver.

Each person has to provide short feedback using these two statements:

- "I like that you… "
- "I wish that you… "

The first question is about appreciating something that people should *continue doing* such as "I like that you challenge our ideas with great questions," or "I like your positive attitude."

The second is about something that you want your colleague to *start or stop doing,* such as "I wish you would participate more often," or "I wish your jokes didn't feel like you aren't taking our conversations seriously."

Make sure people don't use the "I wish… " to say something polite like "I wish you continue being as collaborative as you are."

The Pixar-Style Braintrust

Honesty is absolutely critical during the creative development process. Whether your team is trying to solve a problem, develop a new product, or improve the way they work, feedback is critical to help ideas grow.

Pixar practices radical candor as a team. The company believes that honesty is critical to turn their "ugly babies," as company cofounder and president Ed Catmull calls them, into box-office successes. Radical candor requires balancing honest feedback while also caring about individuals.

Pixar refers to their ideas review method as "Braintrusts." Its purpose is "to push toward excellence and root out mediocrity." Catmull considers Braintrusts to be Pixar's culture secret sauce.

A Braintrust is formed of two groups of colleagues that meet periodically. On one side is the team that's working on a movie and requires feedback. The other is a team working on a different film.

The focus of the conversation is to get input on the key elements like the storyline, characters, design, etc. The movie "owners" present their idea to the other team. The givers provide input on the movie; they don't judge or evaluate the people involved.

Most importantly, the other team is there to help, not compete, with their colleagues.

The project owners decide what to do with the feedback received.

Andrew Stanton, *Finding Nemo's* director, compared a Braintrust with a panel of doctors. "If Pixar is a hospital and the movies are the patients, then the Braintrust is made up of trusted doctors."

Pixar has created a psychologically safe culture by encouraging people to share feedback in the open. You can do the same by encouraging different teams to give feedback on each other's projects.

A typical Braintrust addresses

- What is wrong
- What is missing
- What isn't clear
- What doesn't make sense

The Blameless Postmortem

When something goes wrong, most teams quickly jump into the name-blame-and-shame game. Time to shift to a "blameless culture."

 A blameless culture doesn't mean a lack of accountability. On the contrary, when teams care more about solving the root cause of a problem rather than finding someone to blame, they become more responsible.

> The underlying belief of a "just culture" is that mistakes are generally a product of faulty organizational cultures rather than the fault of one or more individuals.

The *Blameless Postmortem* is an exercise practiced by crafts and vintage items e-commerce website Etsy. CEO Chad Dickerson wanted to shift the conversation from "Who's the CEO going to fire?" to learning from mistakes. This practice has helped Etsy employees take more risks and move faster. Dickerson told *Business Insider* : "One of the things I allowed people to do is make mistakes more freely. The best way to learn to ride a bike is to ride the bike and fall down."[90]

Holding a blameless postmortem requires shifting the conversation from pointing fingers to finding out what happened and how you can make it better. Following are some guidelines for facilitating effectively.

Assume good intentions: People usually act based on the information they had at the time. Assume everyone involved acted with the best intentions.

Don't react emotionally: Take a deep breath before you react, then ask the right questions and explore what caused the error.

Focus on facts, not perceptions: Encourage the team to reflect on what actually happened and what they would do differently next time.

Identify causes, not culprits: Move from "who?" to "why?" Understanding the root cause might require more effort, but it will help prevent future mistakes.

Be consistent: This piece of advice comes from Atlassian's playbook: "If one postmortem is blameless and others aren't, the removal of fear and introduction of more openness won't work."

Triad Feedback: Go Slow to Go Fast

This exercise makes it easier for people to open up in smaller groups. The feedback is focused on a particular challenge they bring up, and everyone switches roles from receiver to giver.

The Triad Feedback (or Troika Consulting, the original name used by Liberating Structures) method makes it easier for people to ask for and provide feedback. It works in groups of three, where everyone takes a turn to give and receive feedback based on a personal challenge.

The "client" (receiver) introduces their problem by answering two questions, "What is your challenge?" and "What kind of help do you need (e.g., advice, ideas, listening, or support)?"

Now the client turns their back to their screen, listens to the "consultants" (givers) brainstorm possible solutions, and takes notes. By turning their back on the screen and not talking, the client can actively listen. Also, the consultants can speak more freely as they are not trying to read the client's body language.

Finally, the client turns around, shares what they heard, and thanks the givers.

Repeat until all three people have played the client role.

BUILD CULTURE, ONE NUDGE AT A TIME

Culture is what we do repeatedly. Team rituals not only bring culture to life but can also shape or transform it.

Successful organizations have been using team rituals to bring people together for many years. However, it took a global pandemic for most companies to discover the power of well-designed rituals.

Fannie Mae plays a pivotal role in the housing finance system. The multibillion government-sponsored company provides liquidity, stability, and affordability to the mortgage market. As of 2021, Fannie Mae ranks 25 on the Fortune 500 list of the largest US corporations by revenue.

I learned this when I interviewed Katya Sylvester, a senior manager, to discuss how she builds culture remotely. Her role, she explained to me, is to help technology changes land safely. Her team was already comfortable with interactive technologies and remote work, so adapting to working from home wasn't a big hurdle from an operational standpoint. The challenge was keeping everyone together.

These days, to provide a break from work and to give all the team members a chance to connect on a more human level, they've adopted a "team walk" ritual. They choose a time of the day when everyone goes for a walk around their neighborhood, often with their dogs. They hold a group call at the same time when they can talk about non-work topics and show off their pets. It's a great way to create a connection even though they all work remotely and live in different areas.

Sylvester's team also practices a deeper emotional ritual that became even more significant during the pandemic. Formerly an in-person get-together, her employees meet on MS Teams weekly to talk about spirituality and share personal stories. Everyone reflects on their thoughts from their specific religious viewpoint, using those insights to improve how they work together. This "encouragement ritual" has brought the team together, helping overcome the distance and improving collaboration.

As Sylvester told me during an interview, "This ritual created a space to be better human beings. Now it's easier to ask for help and support. Whatever comes up, the team rises up. Take care of what you need to do; we'll take care of your work."

Sylvester broke into tears when she spoke to me. From battling cancer and celebrating a brother's return from war to losing a loved one and dealing with COVID-19, she appreciates the safe space team members have created to share their authentic selves.

Rituals are an effective way to build a remote team culture. Well-designed team rituals can foster belonging, connect people with culture, and bring remote teams closer. Since the beginning of the pandemic, the need for rituals has become even more significant. Some companies have created new rituals; others have recreated existing rituals to practice them remotely.

I was helping teams design rituals even before the pandemic. Now, having watched so many organizations transition to remote work, my team and I have learned a lot about the power of rituals and how they help build culture at a distance—one nudge at a time.

In the following pages, I will share exactly what a team ritual is, what the benefits are, and how to design the right rituals for your own team.

What Are Rituals, and Why Do They Matter to Virtual Teams?

Many people use the terms "icebreakers," "team-building activities," and "rituals" interchangeably. Although they all are connected, they are not the same.

Frederick Pferdt, chief innovation evangelist at Google, defines rituals as "tangible acts done routinely that carry value and meaning." Rituals are symbolic shared experiences that strengthen bonds, heighten morale, reinforce culture, improve communication, and increase a sense of belonging. Rituals increase social cohesion, aligning the belief system of the individual with the team. Through repetition, they help reinforce positive behaviors and emotions. Team rituals are unique to each company or team culture; they don't make sense to those who aren't part of the group.

According to IDEO's CEO Tim Brown, "Rituals create a constant nudging so that, over time, a culture learns to do something naturally and intuitively." The more a belief system is enacted through ritual, the stronger it becomes.

A ritual enables identity transformation, resulting in a change of behavior. Rituals play a strong part in building performance, which is why sports teams have been practicing them for ages.

The All Blacks are not just the best rugby team in history; they're one of the most successful sports teams *ever*. They have an all-time winning percentage of 77.41% over 580 international matches. The All Blacks' most famous ritual is the Haka, a ceremonial dance inherited from the Maori culture that is meant to intimidate rivals before a game.[91] However, New Zealand's national rugby team practices another ritual that is not as well-known but just as meaningful.

This one happens behind closed doors and has nothing to do with brute force and intimidation; in an act known as "sweeping the sheds," the All Blacks clean their locker room after every practice and match. This team ritual is designed to show thanks, build humility, and reinforce that all members are equal.

 Rituals require repetition to create a real impact. The more they are enacted, the more natural and organic they become.

People can participate in rituals simultaneously or at different times, meaning that different locations or different time zones don't need to get in the way of powerful rituals. Before the pandemic, Zappos's employees enjoyed a company garden in which the harvest was shared among employees. During the pandemic, Zappos sent employees an herb garden kit and encouraged them to post photos of their gardens and the food they cooked, keeping the sense of community alive.

The in-person ritual was synchronous, the virtual version was asynchronous, but both contributed to a shared sense of community.

So, what's the difference between rituals, habits, and routines?

Habits and routines have one thing in common with rituals: repetition. However, rituals require more effort and consciousness, as shown in the chart below.

The Nature of Habits, Routines, and Rituals

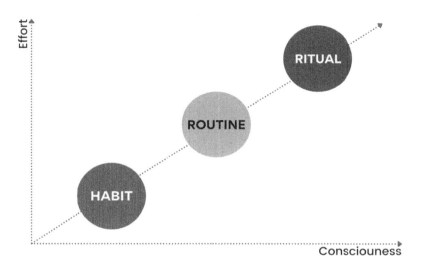

Habits are small acts that we perform on a regular basis without thinking. Brushing your teeth is a perfect example. It's something that you learned when you were a kid and by now, probably do it almost unconsciously.

Routines require an extra level of effort and awareness. For example, an exercise routine involves changing your clothes, warming up, exercising, stretching, taking a shower, etc. You have to put a little more effort into planning it and thinking it through.

A happy hour on Friday, for example, is not a ritual but a routine. It takes some planning, sure, but it doesn't really shape culture. The same happens with some agile practices like retrospectives or check-ins. They are not rituals per se because they lack profound emotional meaning. They are functional, not emotional in nature.

What Are the Key Characteristics of a Ritual?

Unlike habits and routines, team rituals require more effort and consciousness. They are defined by the following five characteristics:

1. Rituals require a trigger

Different elements can trigger a ritual. For example, a specific date or time: every Monday at 8 a.m. or at the beginning of our weekly action meeting. Internal events (when a new hire joins our team or when we finish a project) or external events (when clients congratulate the team or our product receives an award) can also act as a trigger.

When exploring new rituals, consider what will trigger them, such as an event or a specific day/time.

2. Rituals have a beginning, middle, and end

In cultural anthropology, a ritual is a journey in which an individual leaves one group or state to join another. Each rite of passage involves three clear steps: beginning, middle, and end.

An example is Airbnb's human tunnel. New employees start their journey at one end of a tunnel made by all employees. The middle, going through the tunnel, represents the transition from one state to another. Finally, they come out the other side, feeling welcomed. They have transformed from "new hire" to "one of us."

Rituals are metaphors. When creating yours, consider the storytelling arc—beginning, middle, and end—to craft the experience/story.

3. Rituals transform behavior

Rituals not only increase belonging but also transform mindsets and behaviors.

For a client suffering from analysis paralysis, we created a ritual called "On Air." When anyone notices that the team is spiraling and failing to "land" on a decision, any member could turn on the "on air" sign during a Zoom call. Similar to what happens in a podcast or radio program, it's a signal that people must stop preparing and go live.

When designing a ritual, define the emotional reward: How do you want the team to feel after completing the ritual?

4. Rituals occur with a particular frequency

Culture is what we do repeatedly. Team rituals help bring your company culture to life over and over by continually enacting a behavior that reminds your team members who they are, how they play, and why they want to work together.

The frequency of a ritual depends on its nature and trigger. Atlassian holds regularly scheduled weekly "Slack Stand-Ups," but their "Brown Bag Sessions," informal learning meetings over lunch, occur whenever there's a need.

Rituals require repetition. Your team will see the benefits as they practice theirs over time.

5. Rituals play a symbolic, transformational role

Unlike a Friday happy hour with our colleagues (a routine), rituals create deeper connections. Not all rituals are equally symbolic. However, most are very meaningful for team members who are part of this collective experience.

Zappos offers a "Pay to Quit" bonus to new employees—people must choose between the tempting offer of getting a check and leaving, or saying no to $4,000 and staying. A large majority reject the offer. This rite of passage separates true Zapponians from those who don't belong.

Use the Design a Team Ritual Canvas to design your team's ritual.

Use the following QR code to download your free copy.

171

RITUALS CHANGE BEHAVIOR (REALLY)

 Rituals do much more than create belonging. They are powerful because they create awareness of the mindsets and behaviors that we want to change.

Anthropologist Clifford Geertz said, "The world as lived and the world as imagined turn out to be the same world." Rituals give teams a sandbox to play and experiment in. Most importantly, they help address issues in a nonthreatening way.

Here are five key areas of opportunities for developing team rituals:

1. Get to Know Your Team Members

Creating belonging and connection are critical for remote teams, especially when members join a new team without meeting people in person.

Build cohorts

Being part of a group makes it easier to go through experiences such as onboarding and makes it easier for everyone to support each other. Miro onboards remote employees in cohorts to help build strong relationships.[92] It makes people feel welcomed and part of the company culture, history, and strategy.

The best and worst

Some people don't want to get too personal. However, you can still get to know them more personally by talking about work. At Liberty IT, employees use a series of questions like "Who was your best colleague and why?" and "Who was your worst boss ever and why?"

Meet each other's loved ones

We are our relationships. Rituals can facilitate connection by introducing colleagues' loved ones: pets, babies, and anything in between.

As I mentioned in Step 1, GitLab team members host "Juice Box" chats, bringing employees' children, grandchildren, and other family members together. At BetterCloud, employees like to show off their pets when they have a video call to strengthen personal relationships among team members.

2. Celebrate Your Culture

Team rituals are perfect for recognizing people and strengthening bonds.

Unsung hero

Have the team vote and nominate a team member who has gone the extra mile, especially those who did so without bragging about it. For example, the shy person who contributed the most, or someone who went outside their comfort zone.

Graduation ceremonies

Welcoming new team members is a critical celebration for every team, especially when people work remotely. Create a small, virtual ceremony where new hires can introduce themselves and get to know their colleagues. Create a team map where everyone's profile is available.

Send a welcome package

The fact that people work from home doesn't mean they can't still get some nice gifts from their new employer. Cupcakes hold significance for Dropbox; its fifth core value—delight—is represented by a picture of a smiling cupcake. Every new employee receives an unlabeled box with a recipe and ingredients to bake their own.

3. Reinforce Positive Behaviors

Team rituals can be used to acknowledge and reward your employees for their work and effort. Well-constructed rituals reinforce the behavior you'd like to see more of.

Regain focus

At Heiligenfeld, a German company specializing in holistic health care, the "Who will ring the bell today?" ritual creates a pause when a meeting is going off track. When ground rules are not respected, the sound of the bell invites participants to reflect on their own behaviors. "Am I in service of the topic we are discussing? Am I adding value or being a distraction?" The meeting restarts with a more effective mindset.

Show appreciation

Southwest Airlines, a regional airline in the US, practices Cultural Blitzes, unexpected events in which a group of employees show their appreciation to flight crews. This ritual includes giving them snacks and good wishes for the day ahead. The key surprise includes cleaning the plane between flights, usually the responsibility of the crew members who were on the plane.

Celebrate failure

Many organizations have rituals aimed at increasing mistake tolerance and developing a learning culture. Tata Motors, the Indian automotive company, believes that mistakes are goldmines. Ratan Tata, former chair of the Tata Group, created a prize for the best-failed idea called "Dare to Try."

At Spotify, teams have regular "Fail-fikas" (*fika* is the Swedish word for having a coffee and a chat together). This ritual encourages people to share their mistakes and learn from each other's errors.

Celebrate contributions

The "Small Moments Jar" team ritual is another way to recognize everyone's contributions. Create a virtual jar in which teammates can drop a sticky note outlining something extraordinary a colleague did. From helping out on a deadline to learning a new skill or organizing a virtual birthday celebration—everything counts. Once a week, the jar gets "opened," and each person shares their notes, acknowledging the person who earned the glory.

4. Increase Belonging

Doing things together in a particular way increases belonging and trust among virtual teams. Here are some ideas:

Create a team playlist

Nothing brings us together—or sets us apart—like music. Define different themes and have each colleague recommend a song to build a playlist that not only represents personal preferences but also creates a shared identity.

Virtual teams contests

Creating friendly competitions between various teams from the same company reinforces belonging and also breaks down silos. Organize cross-company contests for "Best team photo," "Coolest team pet," or "Best team virtual background," to name a few.

Hold a virtual bonfire

Hotjar holds weekly events that get employees together in an intimate and casual environment: virtual bonfires. It's a moment to connect, discuss interesting topics, and share new ideas. Sometimes, special guests join and spark interesting conversations around the warmth of a virtual bonfire.

Grab a coffee with the CEO

Real conversations increase transparency, which in itself is associated with trust and lower turnover. GoTo's CEO hosts weekly virtual cafés that all employees can join. They are recorded so no one misses the conversation. During these café chats, employees come up with suggestions and ideas. All the progress is documented on a website where people can see what was said and what the company is doing to provide employees with a better experience.

5. Team Rituals to Improve Virtual Collaboration

Well-designed team rituals can help improve participation, one nudge at a time.

Run a sparring session

This structured way to get feedback comes from Atlassian's playbook. Just as martial artists or boxers don't train alone, a sparring session with your colleagues will improve your game. Share your work in a safe setting and get quick, honest feedback from the diverse perspectives of your colleagues.

Call out interruptions

Interruptions have skyrocketed in virtual environments. This ritual invites people to cut them out. To ensure that all voices are heard, create a visual ritual to call out interrupters. We use scissors in our workshops so participants can put them in front of their camera to call out those who are "cutting off" their colleagues.

Design detention

This ritual by Alastair Simpson, design lead at Atlassian, helps remote teams overcome constant interruptions. Teams need quality time and focus to tackle wicked problems. Design detentions are partial or full days where teams get together in the same virtual space to work without interruptions. Emails, Slack, meetings, and one-on-ones are banned.

Rituals are symbolic shared experiences that strengthen connections, communication, and a sense of belonging. Through repetition, they help reinforce desired beliefs and behaviors.

> *When designing a ritual, don't overthink it, just build the first thing you can, then move to more sophisticated versions later.*
> —Tim Brown, CEO and president of IDEO

Recap

STEP 3: REIGNITE BELONGING

A solid sense of belonging is vital for building a strong remote culture.

Psychological safety promotes courageous conversations and innovation.

You can consciously help your team advance up the Psychological Safety Ladder.

Building a culture of regular, peer-to-peer feedback helps the team improve performance, addressing conflict before it escalates.

Team rituals strengthen bonds, help align the individual with the team, and improve behavior in a nonthreatening way.

The following exercise will help you help your team climb higher on the Psychological Safety Ladder and create a culture of belonging.

YOUR TURN: REIGNITE PSYCHOLOGICAL SAFETY

Use the Psychological Safety Ladder Canvas to map and understand how your team is faring, identify areas of opportunities, and prioritize action.

Set up the right environment by preparing the team for the session. Most importantly, share the purpose of the session: to assess how safe the culture of the team is and identify specific areas to tackle.

This task has three steps:

- Facing the ladder
- Assessing each level
- Repairing the steps

You can download a free copy of the Psychological Safety Ladder using the QR code below.

1. Face the Ladder

Have each member assess the level of psychological safety within the team, reflecting on the different statements per level. They should evaluate each of the statements using the following color code:

Yes   = green
Maybe   = yellow
No   = red

The MURAL template has sticky notes in yellow. Participants can keep them in yellow or turn their color to red or green, depending on their assessment.

Another option that works both for in-person and virtual sessions is to use Mentimer or Slido for anonymous voting; the results are captured live so everyone can see the final assessment.

Debrief with your team:

- What steps are green, yellow, or red?
- Green steps: What success stories do we have? What can we learn?
- Yellow steps: What will it take to make these green?
- Red steps: What's preventing us from doing better?
- How can each team member contribute?

2. Assess Each Level

As a result of the previous assessment, you can identify how well your team is doing level by level and determine which are strong, weak, or broken. This analysis will help you prioritize your focus. Logically, you can't do well at Level 2 if you have issues at Level 1. You have to improve the lower levels before going up the ladder.

Use the results of the initial activity to assess each level: Welcome, Courageous Conversations, and Innovation. Which one is strong, weak, or broken?

As a rule of thumb, 75+% is strong, 50-75% is weak, and <50% is broken.

Facilitate a group discussion

What are the observations? What are the surprises and contradictions? How do people feel about it? What makes them excited to help improve psychological safety? What makes them unmotivated to tackle the issues at hand?

It's important to avoid finger-pointing or guilting. The purpose of this conversation is not to rehash what's broken but to identify areas for building a stronger team culture.

3. Repair the Steps

It doesn't matter how many steps are broken. Focusing is critical. Fix one at a time. Start with one crucial step or an area where you can achieve a quick win and build momentum.

Do you want to increase participation in meetings? Do your team members need to know each other better? Do you need to make it okay for people to ask for help? It's impossible to fix everything at once. Choose one step and focus the conversation on how to repair it.

First, allow time for self-reflection. Have each individual write what behavior they think they and others should have inside a "safety net." Then ask them to capture which ones they don't want.

Once everyone has finished, invite team members to put the "behaviors we want" inside the safety net—what you want "in." Then they should put the "behaviors we don't want" outside the safety net.

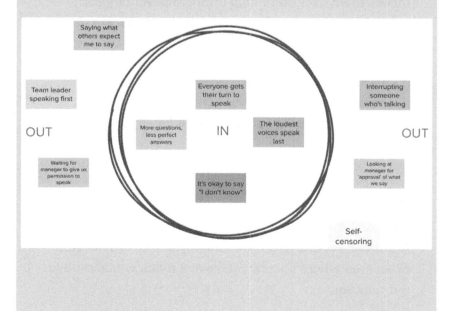

Facilitate a group discussion. Ensure the team is aligned in what they want "in" and "out." This is a moment for everyone to be honest and sign a team contract.

Go back to the activities on creating rituals and changing your feedback systems that I shared earlier and choose the ones that will help you tackle your specific challenges. Monitor progress, and once one step is repaired, move on to fix the next one.

RETHINK
COLLABORATION

STEP 4

OUR IDEA OF COLLABORATION IS BROKEN

For decades, business experts have glorified "collaboration" as a way for organizations to be more productive and innovative. However, there was never a lot of evidence that collaboration was the key to either innovation or productivity—and now there's even less.

A meta-analytic review of over 800 teams shows that individuals are more likely to generate a higher number of original ideas when they *don't* interact with others.[93] The push for hyper-collaboration drains people. It creates collaboration burnout and may be just as likely to undermine performance as to enhance it.

Leaders' obsession with hyper-collaboration can quickly undermine performance, as research by Morten T. Hansen, professor of management at UC Berkeley, shows.[94]

Collaboration can slow down teams and projects; sometimes the cost is not worth the time and effort.

As Hansen explains, "Too often a business leader asks, 'How can we get people to collaborate more?' That's the wrong question. It should be, 'Will collaboration on this project create or destroy value?'"

The key to building a thriving culture of collaboration is knowing when collaboration isn't necessary. The traditional approach to collaboration is broken. Not only we were sold on the notion that collaboration is all or nothing—either you collaborate or you don't—we've been programmed to think that collaboration only happens in real-time.

There are many ways of working that don't require collaborating with others synchronously or, for that matter, collaborating at all. To thrive in the new reality of work, you must rethink collaboration. That's exactly what happened to serial entrepreneurs Torben Friehe and Yann Leretaille.

The two high-school dropouts were certain about one thing when they founded 1aim in 2012: "We are never going to go remote."

1aim was a building-management SaaS software company based in Berlin, Germany. From mechanical engineering and electrical engineering to backend and frontend, everyone in the company had to work the same schedule in the same office. The cofounders were adamant that all employees had to work locally and denied any requests, even temporary ones, for remote work. They told me: "As an engineering-focused company, we believed that great technology and culture could only happen under one roof. We didn't even hire freelancers. We wanted the whole team to work in the office, full-time."

One of the main reasons was the complexity of the work. Leretaille recalls, "We need all these different disciplines, all these people to interact a lot. We spent years building a culture of people respecting each other, really cooperating, and we thought it definitely helped build that environment by being in the same place, one schedule."

The company was an engineer's paradise, with a big electrical lab and a mechanical lab housing everything from 3D printers to prototyping machines. The founders couldn't imagine reproducing and scaling that experience in people's homes. Would they be sending prototypes back and forth between people's homes so everyone could do their part? "We didn't know how to do that. Maybe some other companies have figured it out, but that wasn't our case. That's why remote for us was never an option," Friehe recounted.

Fast forward to 2021: Friehe and Leretaille sold 1aim and moved to San Francisco to start a new company, Wingback, a pricing plan management platform. The first question they asked themselves was: "Do we do it again the same way we did?"

This time, the entrepreneurs decided to go fully remote from day one.

So, what changed? It was pretty clear that hiring a qualified team in a single location would be harder than in the past. The pandemic was definitely a barrier. But, most importantly, people had gotten used to the flexibility of working from home.

"We were very afraid about having to lead a team remotely," Leretaille was vulnerable enough to admit. "But we realized that this time we had to do it differently, and we decided to design a remote-first culture from the get-go." In fact, their first hire was a fractional head of remote. The cofounders realized that managing a distributed team would be a huge challenge and would require intentional design.

Friehe and Leretaille have always believed in hiring global talent. Ten years ago, that meant relocating people to Berlin so their employees could work together. With Wingback, they were able to forgo the complexities and costs of relocation but had another challenge: How would they collaborate effectively when members were working from different places and time zones?

The first strategic decision was adopting an async-first approach. That required setting up a knowledge base, intentionally defining the culture, and codifying expected behaviors. They defined the new ways of working long before their first employees started.

One crucial lesson from their journey is that we cannot apply the same way of thinking to the new reality of work.

This insight is true for you, too, whether you are managing a hybrid team or a fully remote one. There's no one-size-fits-all solution.

In Step 4: Rethink Collaboration, we'll discuss what it means to default to async-first, and I'll invite you to explore the different ways of collaborating—or not collaborating—in a hybrid or remote world.

THE PROBLEM WITH REAL-TIME

Collaboration burnout was already a problem long before the pandemic started.[95] The globalization and digitalization of the economy were forcing people to collaborate more, even outside their organizations, increasing the number of meetings, calls, emails, Slack messages—you name it. The result was collaboration overload.

The pandemic shone a spotlight on the problems of an "always-on" culture as the average employee clocked in an extra 2.5 hours a day after moving to remote work.[96] We are working more than ever before; 40% of people have experienced burnout in some shape or form. The lack of clear boundaries to the day, like commuting to and from work, has made it more difficult to switch off.

Prioritizing input over outcome is not helping either, as I discussed in Step 1. When presenteeism and workload are success metrics, employees are afraid to step away. If you switch off, people think you're lazy. You feel guilty if you can't be available 24/7. But just because you *can* always be on doesn't mean you *should* be. If you never take time to wind down, motivation, productivity, and creativity suffer.

And it doesn't take much—even a minor interruption can derail your personal time. A peek at an email distracts you from enjoying dinner. You hit reply and your attention goes to the screen as you anxiously wait for an answer. One task leads to another and you're back in work mode. The time you're supposed to use to unwind ends up contributing to more burnout.

Research shows that long hours backfire for both people and companies.[97] Always being "on" increases conflict between our work and personal lives.[98] Reviewing emails outside of regular working hours significantly increases stress,[99] while compulsive internet use is a symptom of workaholism.[100]

The always-on culture produces harmful long-term effects. When employees are overworked and overstressed, they become unhappy and demotivated. This leads to an increase in absenteeism and turnover, harming productivity and driving inequality in the workplace, especially, as we discussed in Step 1, for women.

 This always-on mentality has always clashed with people's needs; now it clashes with their expectations as well. The Great Resignation is turning into

> the Great Reshuffle. People are not just leaving the
> workforce but also reconfiguring their relationship
> with work.

Globally, nearly seven in ten respondents said hybrid is their preferred work environment. People want flexibility, not just in where they work but also when. While 78% of all survey respondents say they want location flexibility, nearly all (95%) want schedule flexibility.

Those are some of the key findings from the global Pulse survey conducted by Future Forum, a consortium launched by Slack, consisting of more than 10,000 knowledge workers from the US, Australia, France, Germany, Japan, and the UK.[101] The message is loud and clear. The employees who are not satisfied with their current job schedule flexibility will look for something else.

As Future Forum Executive Leader and Slack Senior Vice President Brian Elliott told me, "The pandemic accelerated a lot of trends that were already in place. It invited us to question conventional wisdom, dramatically changing the expectations of employees."

Elliott pointed out a disconnect between what leaders want and what employees demand: "Seventy-five percent of executives in the survey say they want employees to be in the office three or more days a week. However, only 37% of individual contributors want to be in the office as much."

The people who are more supportive of fully returning to the physical office—and watercooler conversations—are those who were successful in that environment. However, Elliott observed, "There's zero academic evidence about the effectiveness of watercooler conversations. Research shows that if you are ten feet apart from your colleagues, you are not having conversations with them."

Resolving the disconnect between employer expectations and worker needs, between the demands of the workplace and the realities of our personal lives, requires rethinking how teams collaborate and communicate in a hybrid workplace.

BALANCING SYNCHRONOUS AND ASYNCHRONOUS WORK

Traditionally, collaboration has been understood as something that needs to happen synchronously, with everyone reviewing information, making decisions, or brainstorming together. We saw a huge increase in workload when companies were forced to work remotely yet with a synchronous mindset. The result was an overload of Zoom meetings, shorter breaks, and an expectation that employees would be available outside regular working hours.

But it doesn't have to be like that. Collaboration is what we want to *achieve* together—it unites us around a shared future—but it doesn't always require that team members *work* together. Dividing and conquering a project is also a form of collaboration.

Three elements define successful collaboration:

Why we do it: the impact we want to achieve together—the team's purpose and goal. Having a shared purpose and goal drive effective collaboration, even if each team member is working independently. However, a team that is not aligned is not really collaborating even if its members are sharing a task, space, or process.

What we do: activities, tasks, and actions, including the roles each team member fulfills.

How we do it: process, methods, and rules, including how we meet and make decisions.

In synchronous collaboration, everyone interacts in real-time in online or in-person meetings, instant messaging, or via Zoom. Asynchronous collaboration, on the other hand, takes place when interactions can be time-shifted, such as uploading documents or annotations to shared workspaces or making contributions to a wiki.

Asynchronous communication adapts best to flexible schedules and relieves the pressure of having to respond immediately. Instead, people can respond at their own pace without interrupting their flow, creating a better collaboration across different time zones.

Increasingly, organizations will need to default to asynchronous rather than synchronous collaboration if they want to be successful. Defaulting to async goes beyond getting rid of meetings or synchronous communication; it requires redefining how team members will make work happen at their own pace.

Zach Holman, one of the first developers at remote GitHub, wrote about the benefits of asynchronous communication: "Asynchronous communication means I can take a step out for lunch and catch up on transcripts when I get back. Asynchronous communication means I can ask my coworker a question and not worry about bothering her since she'll get back to me when she's available. Asynchronous communication means I can go to rural Minnesota and feel like I'm working from the office like normal."

Gartner Research Director Alexia Cambon emphasized the link between intentional collaboration and innovation: "Our research shows that teams of knowledge workers who collaborate intentionally are nearly three times more likely to achieve high team innovation than teams that do not use an intentional approach." [102]

Distributed teams can work in four ways, based on whether they're in the same location and working at the same time. This adds complexity but also provides additional opportunities for teams to explore more effective ways of working. Most importantly, it allows them to strategize whether to work together from the same place or from different locations.

The image below captures the four possible scenarios:

- Synchronous and physically present at the office
- Synchronous in distributed locations
- Asynchronous and physically present at the office
- Asynchronous in distributed locations

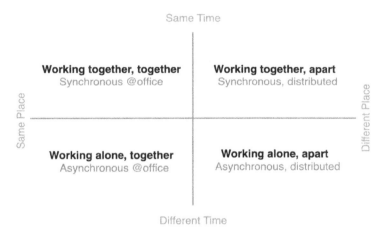

Recently, "asynchronous" has often become part of business jargon, unfortunately, presented as a quick fix. However, it's not a one-size-fits-all approach, and hybrid collaboration is more challenging than most people realize. For starters, many organizations don't come from a culture of collaboration; they just force people to work together, without intentional design and often, with poor results.

An executive from a major US retailer recently admitted this to me, "We romanticized the idea of group brainstorming in the office. But, looking at it from a distance, that magical experience was just an illusion. The outcome was usually disappointing."

Regardless, smart collaboration happens by design, not chance. The new reality of work provides a unique opportunity to dramatically change the way people collaborate. You must decide when and under what circumstances async makes sense for your situation and adapt it to your team's situation.

In the following section, we'll look at the six modes of collaboration that distributed teams can use to begin building an intentional culture of collaboration.

SIX MODES OF COLLABORATION FOR DISTRIBUTED TEAMS

The hybrid workplace has made it more critical than ever to intentionally identify the different types of work, encouraging people to switch from one to another as needed. Most collaboration models, however, remain office-centric.

A 2012 study by furniture company Herman Miller uncovered ten modes of work.[103] The first six—chat, converse, co-create, huddle, show and tell, and warm-up/cool-down are "together" work modes that consist of collaborative activities between two or more people. The last three—process and respond, create, and contemplate—are done alone and consist of focused, individual activities.

Workplace research by the Gensler architecture and design consulting firm uncovered a simpler model consisting of four modes of working: focus, collaboration, learning, and socialization.[104]

Building on those two models, I developed a framework to unlock the possibilities of a hybrid, nonoffice-centric workplace. This approach is based on two different axes:

- "Me Time" versus "We Time"—activities we perform at our own pace and time versus those that we do together.
- "Deep Work" versus "Casual Work"—activities that require more concentration, quality time, and focus versus those that require less.

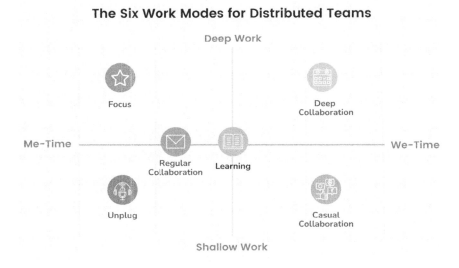

The Six Work Modes for Distributed Teams

This gives us the following six work modes:

1. Focus work
2. Deep collaboration
3. Regular collaboration
4. Learning
5. Casual collaboration
6. Unplugged

Let's have a closer look at each one.

Work Mode 1: Focus Work

This is deep, heads-down work. Focus work encompasses tasks such as strategizing, planning, research, idea genera-tion, or content creation. To produce the absolute best work you're capable of, you need to commit to focus and do your job without distractions—no emails, no Slack, no meetings.

The ability to perform focus work is a critical yet rare skill in the knowledge economy. Cal Newport, author of *Deep Work*, calls it "a superpower in our increasingly competitive twenty-first-century economy."[105] Research at UC Berkeley validates the importance of focus work: people reported being 43% more productive when they could carve out a daily block of uninterrupted time.[106]

If you spend most of your time in a distractive, frenetic environment (casual work), you reduce your critical think-ing capacity and simply won't be able to produce your highest-quality work. Fortunately, you can create "zones" for distraction-free work by designing your routine, habits, and rituals.

Mars Wrigley's global packaging team has instituted "Focus Fridays." All team members block out their calendars, no meetings are allowed, and people can do focused, uninterrupted work. Just as important, Focus Fridays create space to wind down the workweek and smoothly transition into the weekend.

William Singleton of Mars Wrigley told me how he came up with the idea: "Getting in the car to go to the office or back from work was a natural boundary. Originally, I didn't recognize it. Once I found myself boundlessly working, I realized I had to recreate an artificial version of the commute. Doing something before working, like going for a walk or taking the dog out, helps me create a transition state of mind. That personal experience inspired me to block time for all my team to do focus work."

The majority of your time should be allocated to doing deep work.

Status: Unavailable and unreachable.

Work Mode 2: Deep Collaboration

This is similar to focus work but in a team setting. Unlike most meetings and team interactions, there's no room for distractions or multitasking. Whether the team is co-creating or making a decision, everyone is focused on accomplishing one single task together. Deep collaboration is vital to advance new ideas and projects—it's the most complex, yet rewarding, type of collaboration.

The benefits of deep collaboration include fostering creativity, aligning team members, accelerating decision-making, increasing big-picture thinking, and integrating diverse perspectives.

Unfortunately, few realize the importance of creating the right space for focus work as a team. That's why design sprints have gained momentum—they are purposefully immersive and collaborative. A team is "locked in a room" for a week to work on just one project.[107]

This is the type of collaboration for which it makes the most sense to be physically in the same place. If team members are going to spend a few days working together focusing on a single project, being in the same room creates a deeper shared experience.

Front line health care workers, clinicians, technicians, facilities professionals, etc., are problem-solvers, but the all-consuming attention required by their work, coupled with the notoriously siloed nature of health care, means that best practices often remain a secret. The Illinois Hospital Association and innovation consultancy Do Tank partnered to run a series of design sessions and turned people who have never met before into true collaborators.

"These sessions provide participants with direct access to people who had been down that road before," Matthew Kelly, partner at Do Tank told me. "Being able to talk to folks who have been in your shoes and made mistakes is fantastic. People can experiment together and get feedback in real-time."

Status: Unavailable and unreachable except for those who are part of the experience

Work Mode 3: Regular Collaboration

Regular collaboration mode includes regular meetings, team huddles, and process and response—the work generated by work. In this mode, you are (or are at least, expected to be) in continuous interaction with others. Think of the feedback loop of emails, chat messages, calls, quick chats, and other interactions that drive work forward.

This is where team magic often goes to waste. Regular collaboration is necessary, but if not carefully monitored, it can bog your team down in busywork.

This is an excellent opportunity to default to asynchronous collaboration—let people respond at their own pace. Also, set clear rules of engagement: tell staff what the best medium is for which type of issue and the expected response time for each. One good option is to block out a standard time for collaboration, making it easier to prevent interruptions.

Leaders at leading German publishing company Gruner + Jahr believe in self-efficacy and provide employees the freedom to manage their work schedules. However, the company has designated ten a.m. to three p.m. as collaboration time—this is the only time that meetings and quick calls are allowed. Trying to schedule something beyond that period is out of bounds. In an emergency, leaders ask if people can shuffle things around rather than "invade" their calendars.

Status: Available at your own pace/discretion or within shared collaboration time.

Work Mode 4: Learning

This work mode is about acquiring new knowledge or skills via education, experience, or observation and may include mentorship, show and tell, experimentation, book clubs, and role-switching. It is vital for acquiring, transferring, and applying new ideas. Learning expands not just knowledge but also horizons and possibilities. The learning mode requires a mid-level of work and can happen at both an individual and collective level.

Just like sports teams spend most of their time practicing, teams in the workplace need to spend time together to experiment with new behaviors, learn from feedback, and prepare to deal with new challenges. Companies need to make space to encourage and reward learning.

Getting new employees up to speed is a key learning opportunity. Social media toolkit Buffer implemented a system to welcome their new hires in two key areas: the "culture buddy" helps the new hire learn and understand the company culture, while the "role buddy" helps the hiring manager draft the onboarding plan, acts as a mentor, and becomes the go-to person to support the new employee.

Other companies have moved their training programs online, as in the case of Volvo, discussed in Step 3. This has provided flexibility and integration. Self-paced training makes it easier for people to develop new skills around their schedules. However, not every training should happen on me time. Developing team skills like adopting collective feedback practices requires that people learn and practice together.

Status: Always open to learning; formal training must be scheduled.

Work Mode 5: Casual Collaboration

This mode of work includes small, impromptu interactions that help build interpersonal relationships and spark new ideas. The benefits of serendipitous encounters are exaggerated—there's no evidence that they boost innovation, while "meetings after the meeting" and "watercooler conversations" are usually exclusive and often promote gossip and backbiting.[108]

However, casual encounters play a significant role in most teams by strengthening social bonds and shared values that enable trust and teamwork. The idea, therefore, is not to recreate the watercooler but to create a better version of it.

Well-designed casual collaboration plays a more significant role than simply bringing people together. It's the foundation of substantial social capital, building the base for deep collaboration. This type of collaboration often begins with a social focus that then sparks an idea or uncovers issues to be addressed.

Virtual coffee chats create opportunities to socialize with colleagues without talking about work. Social calls with no set agenda strengthen bonding and also facilitate resolving simple issues. Hobby-specific Slack channels are great to build connections among people with similar interests.

The Future Forum team at Slack has a five to ten-minute social query at the beginning of their weekly meeting during which they ask lighthearted questions like, "Which winter sports would you want to compete in?" It sparks social connection and fun and helps team members get to know each other better.

Status: Spontaneous availability—make it optional for people to participate.

Work Mode 6: Unplugged

This mode of work is when your mind, brain, and body take a break. It might mean pausing to recharge or stopping work altogether.

Working remotely has added to our anxieties, stresses, and workload, with burnout the frequent result. Relaxing, reflecting, and recharging are vital for creating the energy that allows us to tackle focus work or deep collaboration.

The unplugged mode is about designing a space to wind down and let your mind wander. It could be talking a walk in the middle of the day, exercising, meditating, doing something fun with your colleagues, or simply not working. Unplugging doesn't just mean taking a break from work but making sure you're disconnected from distractions such as email, chat, or social media.

Eurich believes that it's imperative to have more honest conversations about levels of burnout. "You can't just fix it with a three-day weekend," she told me. "Leaders should help team members manage their workload, build boundaries, and coach them to create practices to stay healthy, both mentally and physically."

Status: Unavailable and unreachable.

DEFAULT TO ASYNC

If you google "Asynchronous work," you'll get thousands of articles with titles like "The future of work is asynchronous" or "Why you should be working asynchronously in 2022."

I'm a believer in defaulting to asynchronous work, but before I discuss the how, I want to address the hype. The shift toward asynchronous-first is not always easy. It requires a huge cultural shift.

First, the majority of the advice on this kind of transition comes from fully remote companies, most of which are in tech. They may have good lessons to share, but you need to adapt those lessons to your own culture and business.

Second, "default to async" doesn't mean getting rid of meetings or all synchronous forms of collaboration altogether. Moving toward a more asynchronous company can help employees produce better work; however, there are times when synchronous communication works best.

Third, and most importantly, the shift toward async requires a culture of trust, autonomy, flexibility, and respect. (I address the different levels in detail in Step 5: Release Agility). Leaders must trust that employees will get the work done even if they are not as visible as they used to be. People need the freedom to decide to collaborate or not, according to what helps them do the best work. Teams need to have the flexibility to create their own cadence, allowing team members to co-create the best approach. Last, managers must respect people's choices and their time.

You can start by understanding the benefits of synchronous and asynchronous work. Remote Work Prep founder Marissa Goldberg says, "If you target the activities toward the benefits of each, it becomes easier to do the shift."

Synchronous communication has two main benefits: speed and connection, making it ideal for one-on-ones, sensitive conversations, and emergencies. Goldberg explained this concept: "Synchronous is super-fast, and we can build connection because we can observe body language and context. What activities can benefit from that? Performance reviews or urgent situations—when there's a big fire and everyone jumps on a call. Also, things that are fast and energetic such as hype calls, casual hangouts, and celebrations."

Asynchronous is more effective for deep work as it gives us the opportunity to think things through before making a decision. Goldberg believes that it's "really effective for the problem-solving, thoughtful decision-making process, for deep work—what should be the majority of a knowledge worker's work."

 Overall, working async creates a more inclusive culture. It's friendlier for teams working across different time zones, creates more space for quiet people, provides time for reflection, and is convenient for parents and caregivers.

Natasha Miller Williams, head of diversity & inclusion at Ferrara, told me, "As a person who's part of multiple marginalized communities—I'm a woman, I'm a woman of color—being at home, I feel safer in my bubble. I don't have to confront some of the experiences I feel when I'm at the office. I now can shutter this 'little door' of the laptop, and I feel safe."

She has heard similar experiences from people from marginalized communities. However, the expert believes there's still a long way to go: "In Zoom, you're not immune to some of those microaggressions that happen in the office. You still have some of the loudest voices still being the loudest. People who participate remotely have to fight harder so those in the room pay attention."

An async-first approach has many benefits. But you have to do it right to leverage its full potential. Let's review the pros and cons of each type of work and then decide which kind of work is best.

Synchronous Communication

Pros:
- Builds rapport with people
- Good for providing critical feedback or discussing sensitive topics
- Good for brainstorming multiple solutions in situations with a lot of unknowns
- Good for aligning the team when there are many variables

- Allows for faster decision-making
- Allows for quick back-and-forth

Cons:
- Creates constant interruptions, adding stress and workload
- Calendars are controlled by others
- Tends to divide the workday into small chunks
- Tends to be less equitable
- Promotes the idea that collaboration requires being in the same room

Asynchronous Communication

Pros:
- Allows people to design their day around work, not emails or messages
- Fewer meetings means more time to actually do things
- Provides a space to reflect, reducing emotionally charged reactions
- Promotes more thoughtful and intentional communication
- Removes the sense that everything is urgent

Cons:
- Can slow down decision-making
- Magnifies trust issues in teams with low psychological safety
- Requires more effort and intentionality
- Because people are often bad at documenting and communicating, there may be more hiccups at the beginning

Gumroad CEO Sahil Lavingia shared an extensive Twitter thread on the benefits his organization has derived from async communication—there's no drama. As communication becomes more thoughtful and less urgent, people are more mindful of how they process information and react.

"Overall, it's a very low-stress environment," Lavingia reflected. "This is possible because everything is documented. And because everyone talks through different text-based mediums, it's easy for people to peek into anything if they're curious. There are also no meetings, so there's no FOMO."[109]

 Discuss with your team the benefits of asynchronous and synchronous communication—and when to use each. The following chart is a good starting point.

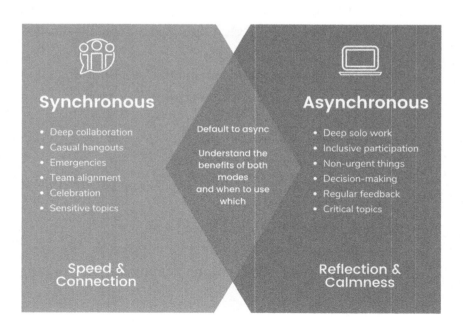

Synchronous

- Deep collaboration
- Casual hangouts
- Emergencies
- Team alignment
- Celebration
- Sensitive topics

Default to async

Understand the benefits of both modes and when to use which

Asynchronous

- Deep solo work
- Inclusive participation
- Non-urgent things
- Decision-making
- Regular feedback
- Critical topics

Speed & Connection

Reflection & Calmness

Mastering asynchronous collaboration increases efficiency and decreases burnout. Even collocated teams can benefit from it; just because people share space doesn't mean they should be constantly interrupted.

Default to asynchronous makes collaboration more inclusive for people across different times zones and provides a safe space for people who need to think to talk. Most importantly, it allows people to be in control of their schedules and not the other way around.

COLLABORATE WITHOUT LOSING YOUR FOCUS

Let go of the idea that your team needs to meet all the time by making team members comfortable with working asynchronously. Block time for deep work, but also protect collaboration time. The following is a list of tips to better balance synchronous and asynchronous communication.

Turn Synchronous Collaboration into Asynchronous

Avoid Zoom fatigue

Reduce the amount of synchronous collaboration by making communication more intentional. Predetermine what needs to be discussed in real-time and what doesn't need an immediate response. Limit video calls to team building, workshops, and brainstorming. Default to asynchronous communication, such as messaging or recorded audio or video, without expecting an immediate response.

Default to asynchronous tools

Prioritize asynchronous communication for teams that are spread across different time zones. Not only is this more inclusive, but it also helps document everything, making information available to everyone at the same time.

Parabol CEO Jordan Husney told me his thoughts on asynchronous tools: "Just a short while ago, it was unfathomable for a team to consider giving up using email for internal communications and switching to a platform like Slack or Microsoft Teams. Companies should stop having meetings to broadcast information and gather feedback, and instead use asynchronous tools to do the same."

Document everything

Create a single source of information that everyone can access and contribute to. You can start with a single company web page or repository in Notion, Google Docs, or software like Jira, GitLab, or GitHub. Everyone on the team should put time and effort into systematically documenting decisions, research, changes to processes, etc.

Documentation provides clarity and consistency, protecting people's focused time. Rather than interrupting your colleagues for information, you can go directly to the single source of truth. Similarly, if there's a conflict, people can direct colleagues to an already-documented agreement instead of relying on personal opinions.

Optimize Synchronous Meetings

Keep meetings small

Successful collaboration requires increased participation. However, productivity has a tipping point beyond which the outcome suffers.

Bob Sutton, organizational psychologist and professor of Management Science and Engineering at Stanford University, says big teams suck.[110] Smaller groups, on the other hand, build a sense of intimacy and safety that opens up participation. Sutton believes that seven (plus or minus two) is the ideal team size.

Amazon follows the two-pizza rule to limit the number of attendees: don't invite more people than you can feed with two pizzas. Keeping meetings small improves collaboration and results.

Keep meetings short

Hour-long meetings are a thing of the past (or should be, anyway). Most meetings should last either 15 or 25 minutes, depending on the topic. The five-minute fraction allows breathing time between meetings.

Being more focused and assigning prework will help shorten existing meetings and save time and distractions. Anything that requires more than 50 minutes should be treated as a workshop, not a meeting.

Design your meetings

Begin with the end in mind. Start with a clear vision of what a successful outcome looks like. Go beyond the agenda to clarify the desired destination and direction.

Have people prepare for the meeting. Prework is a critical step in maximizing live interactions. Define clear roles and let participants know what's expected of them. Consider the mindset: do you want to focus or flare? You don't want a judgmental mindset during a brainstorming session, nor do you want people coming up with creative new ideas just when the team has to make a decision. Assign a facilitator to ensure equal participation, keep the team on track, and design effective conversation.

Integrate Synchronous and Asynchronous Collaboration

Level the playing field

For synchronous meetings, create a space where those who can't attend in person can send their ideas or comments, either recorded via video or in text format, so that everyone can participate.

Tasha Eurich recommends providing options for interaction as introverted people may feel safer asking questions via chat than speaking on video calls.

Create a content sequence

In the in-office world, companies relied heavily on one-time presentations to share new plans or strategies. Now, in a remote environment, they need to create sequences of smaller doses of content in different formats that people can consume on their own time. Moreover, they must become obsessive about communication to prevent misunderstandings. This includes providing context that helps people understand new information and repeating it so that it isn't forgotten.

At Wingback, leaders share live video quarterly updates for all employees, which are also recorded for those who can't attend. They have a follow-up sequence that includes a visual version on Jira, a shorter video, and a written version. Every piece of content provides a different angle and allows employees to choose the format that best suits their preferences.

Create a continuous experience

Synchronous and asynchronous modes aren't opposites; they're more like two sides of the same coin. They need to be integrated and considered as parts of a whole.

At Microsoft in Europe, the team does prework before getting together, including crafting the agenda and meeting flow.

They then meet synchronously to discuss the topics and make decisions. After the meeting, each team member takes care of their parts and informs each other using MS Teams chat. Unless it's really necessary, they don't regroup until it's time to complete the project.

Make synchronous content asynchronous

Make sure people are not excluded from live company events. Record meetings so everyone can watch them later if they aren't able to attend synchronously. Instead of having a meeting, use Loom and record a quick video to share your ideas with your team. Team members can provide feedback after watching it.

Slack records all-hands meetings for people to watch when it's convenient given their time zone and when they have time to digest the presentation properly. Employees can then (asynchronously) ask questions using the Ask Me Anything channel.

Watch out for proximity bias

The majority of executives who want to return fully or almost fully to the office are senior leaders, male, and white, without children at home. In contrast, minority groups and working parents want to work mostly from home. This disconnect creates a huge risk of proximity bias.

Using technology that allows everyone to participate equally helps reduce this risk. Have a facilitator who ensures equal participation and invites those joining remotely to speak first. Level the playing field by having everyone join from their computer, including those at the office. Institute a practice of hand-raising (virtually or physically) to request their turn to speak. Monitor inclusion by having a regular conversation and identifying issues before they become a problem.

Make Meetings Optional

The law of two clicks

Who wants to attend a party where you're forced to show up? Companies should ax all mandatory meetings, and instead allow people to decide for themselves if they will attend.

Make it okay for people to invoke the "law of two clicks," inspired by the Law of Two Feet, which states that anytime you find yourself in any situation where you are neither learning nor contributing, you should use your two feet to move to someplace more productive. If employees feel they are not contributing or learning during a meeting, they can choose to leave the Zoom call (the first click), and confirm their decision (the second click) so that they can put their time and effort into something more productive.

Make meetings a last resort

Whether you're planning a face-to-face event, a Zoom call, or a synchronous brainstorming on Slack, think twice. Does it *need* to be a meeting? Explore all possibilities before hitting send to that calendar invite.

All status meetings should become asynchronous. As Jordan Husney told me, "Eliminating information-sharing meetings off everybody's calendar can save a team several hours a week. Just think about how each person having more focus time would positively impact team performance."

Be flexible

Having a regular meeting on the calendar doesn't mean you always need to have it.

Spotify teams hold daily synchronous meetings, but members can decide each time whether or not it's really necessary to attend. The meeting agenda is flexible and built on the fly (versus predetermined) with input from each of the participants. If there's nothing worth discussing, then the team decides not to meet.

Block your calendar

Timeboxing is a powerful tool for asynchronous-first cultures. It's about blocking different periods of time to work on different things—from focus work to casual collaboration.

Nir Eyal, author, lecturer, and investor known for his best-selling book, *Hooked: How to Build Habit-Forming Products*, wrote about the benefits of timeboxing. "If you don't plan your day in advance—according to your values and your schedule—someone else will plan it for you."[111]

Time is our most precious asset, so be intentional and consistent in its use. Torben Friehe agrees: "I schedule all my meetings in the afternoon so I can keep the beginning of my day free for focused work. In the past, I would take calls and thought it wasn't a big deal, but after some time, I realized that it was a big deal—it really hurt my performance. Now, I avoid calls in the morning at all costs."

Design Your Team Cadence

Turn onboarding into an experience

In the physical office, onboarding was a one-off experience usually managed by HR. In a hybrid workplace, it requires more effort and intentionality. Successful remote onboarding includes small doses of content, a partnership, and a sequence.

Wingback has a sequence that includes an onboarding document, an email to set up Slack and define a personal schedule, a call with the head of remote operations to walk through company policies and processes, an email sequence with an introduction to the different elements of the company culture and how they work, and calls with the founders.

Assigning an onboarding buddy can ease the pain.[112] Earlier, I mentioned Buffer's buddy system for new hires. Microsoft has a similar system and has found that new hires with assigned onboarding buddies show a 36% increase in overall work satisfaction at the 90-day mark.[113]

Establish an in-person connection

Slack has a digital-first approach. Slack (the app) is the new headquarters. It's the main source of communication and information, leveling the playing field for all employees.

However, digital-first doesn't mean "never in person." Most teams at Slack still have large gatherings once a quarter to bring everyone together. The purpose is to spend a couple of days planning in-person and to go out for a meal—nothing replaces the value of eating together.

Some smaller teams at Slack have monthly or weekly in-person meetings, depending on each team's agreement. The sales team meets more frequently than others so junior salespeople can be coached by and learn from senior salespeople.

Share the virtual jet lag

As I mentioned in Step 1, at my consulting firm, Fearless Culture, we alternate our open workshops to adapt the time to attendees from all continents. Sometimes, it's our team who stays until midnight so participants don't have to.

Sharing the pain is the secret sauce for high-performing virtual teams; nothing makes a team stronger than dealing with hardship together. That's one of organizational psychologist David Burkus's key pieces of advice for making a remote team feel like a team.[114]

Considering the different time zones and rotating meeting times accordingly ensures that every teammate gets their fair share of convenient meeting times, late nights, and early mornings. Use online tools to be aware of the different time zones and to find the ones most convenient for everyone. Have deep respect for your colleagues' time zones. Remember, Friday for you may be Saturday for someone else.

Recap

STEP 4: RETHINK COLLABORATION

Collaboration does not need to happen in real-time (often, it doesn't need to happen at all).

A successful hybrid workplace calls for rethinking how teams collaborate and communicate.

Default to async should be the goal, but that doesn't mean getting rid of all synchronous forms of communication.

Smart collaboration happens by design, not chance.

Define the work modes that best suit your team, protecting time for deep work, both individual and collective.

YOUR TURN: RETHINK COLLABORATION

Effective collaboration happens by design, not chance. Organizations that intentionally adopt the six work modes—focus, deep collaboration, regular collaboration, learning, casual collaboration, and unplugged—can achieve greater results, innovation, and teamwork.

Now it's time to put all the insights and ideas that we've discussed into practice by intentionally designing your own team's remote collaboration.

Start by having all participants familiarize themselves with the six modes of work and also the pros and cons of asynchronous and synchronous collaboration.

 Differentiate between "good" and "bad" collaboration. When is collaboration really needed, and when does it become more expensive or slower than people working on their own? The cost of collaboration should always be justified by the outcome.

Session Flow

Kick off the session by discussing the issues related to real-time collaboration and have everyone reflect on and share their personal experiences. This step will set the right mood and help everyone start from a place of empathy. People will acknowledge how vital this conversation is when they reconnect with their own pain.

Invite participants to map the ways the team currently collaborates. They should do this individually first, then consolidate everything into one single board and brainstorm on the pros and cons of the current methods to identify what's working and what's not. Use the tips I shared in the previous section.

After finding some common ground, address communication best practices. Discuss and decide which practices and tools will work best for each type of work.

For example, one client agreed that when collaborating on Anywhere/Anytime projects, team members will use MURAL. Anyone can add ideas and make comments at their own pace, but no one can delete or replace someone else's sticky notes. The selection and elimination process should happen later, when all team members are collaborating at the same time, regardless of location.

Finding the right collaboration approach not only entails considering what's best for a particular activity (decision-making, brainstorming, onboarding new employees, etc.), but also its cost.

The Hybrid Team Canvas is a variant of the Culture Design Canvas framework I shared in the introduction. Use it to capture all the agreements and to map other elements of your hybrid team culture addressed in previous steps like your purpose, priorities, or feedback.

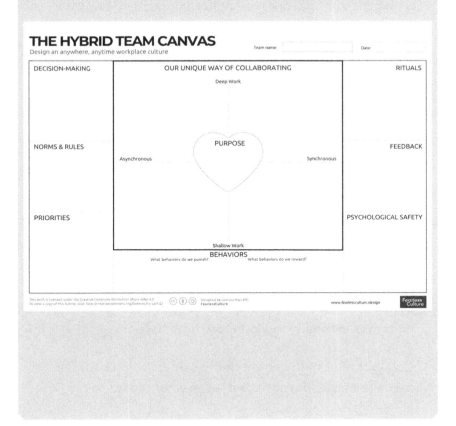

Use the following QR code to download your copy.

What to Watch Out For

Using the wrong work mode(s)for your activities. Use the six modes of work to help your team understand the different needs members have as they move through their working day.

Different types of projects and activities require different approaches. Choose the work modes that work best for each need. Clarify expectations and align your team on how they want to work.

Collaborating when you don't need to

Staying in collaboration mode all the time is bad. You get tired, your work isn't as good, and collaboration suffers. Working together is not always the solution. Distributed teams have discovered the power of asynchronous work and having more time to focus.

Collaboration mode—whether it's deep, regular, or casual—has its purpose, but we are not meant to be there all the time. Is the cost of collaboration worth it? Determine when it makes sense and when it doesn't. Professional facilitation can be very useful in helping your team relearn how to adopt each of the collaboration modes.

Not transitioning from one work mode to another

Transitioning from one mode of work to the other is just as important as transitioning from one meeting to the next. As leadership coach Katia Verresen has said, "People go from meeting to meeting without thinking that one influences their performance or responses in another. Maybe they saw some discouraging data, or had a rough call. We give ourselves zero transition time, and the result is emotional transference."

Not protecting "me-time" modes

Constant interruptions push us back into synchronous work. Even tools like Microsoft Teams have created bigger problems; rather than eliminating email, they're constantly distracting us.

Neuroscientist Lucas Miller explained, "Technology advances usually supplant what has come before but some have just doubled the pain."[115] He sees messaging apps as scary offenders in stopping people from getting their work done.

Protect your unplugged or focus time from others in the same way you block your calendar for meetings.

Test and Iterate

 Collaboration is not always the answer. Discuss the different work modes with your hybrid team.

Choosing the right work mode will not only achieve a better outcome but also reduce unnecessary interruptions and communication overload. Cal Newport wrote, "The future of office work won't be found in continuing to reduce the friction involved in messaging but, instead, in figuring out how to avoid the need to send so many messages in the first place."[116]

Most importantly, be open to experimentation. The first version will never be the final one. Even if you get it right the first time, you'll have to make adjustments as the team, nature of the work, and people's preferences evolve.

RELEASE AGILITY

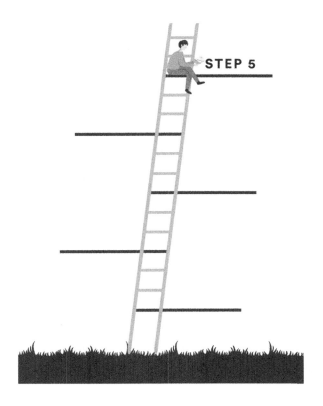

STEP 5

AUTONOMY IS THE NEW ENGAGEMENT

Engagement alone doesn't guarantee exceptional work—autonomy is actually more effective for driving innovative, groundbreaking behavior. Giving employees more control results in great work.[117] That's why Gruner + Jahr, the German publishing company, believes that each team should choose when and where to work.

However, after seeing big announcements from large companies forcing employees back into the office, G+J wanted to validate its approach and asked "Do we have a reason to implement company-wide rules for office presence?"

G+J tasked data scientist Jonas Wolter to answer this question. The mathematician designed a study to correlate employee satisfaction survey responses with how often people are at the office. Basically, was office presence an indicator of job satisfaction?

Mareike Nottrott, HR Manager People & Organizational Development at G+J, told me, "Our research was aimed to see if remote work could harm employee satisfaction or identification. Can we validate that when people work remotely they care less about the company? We didn't find any evidence that working remotely actually harms culture, information exchange, or collaboration."

G+J is not a fully remote company, but a hybrid one. Even though the teams that worked fully remotely were the ones who reported more satisfaction, there were also positive results from those working primarily in the office. Location is not the reason why people produce better results—choice is.

Wolter reported that the study supported G+J's initial hypothesis: "We started the research with one question: Would people want to come back to the office? The answer we have found so far is that there's no one-size-fits-all solution. We couldn't find one single reason to support that we need a company-wide set of rules that define our employees' presence at the office."

Future Forum's research shows a similar pattern: across the board, remote workers reported better experiences than others in areas such as work-life balance, ability to focus, access to resources, and stress.[118] Hybrid appears to be the model of choice. Not only do people report better results than in-office-only workers, but it also provides flexibility.

"It's past time to move beyond the 'remote versus office' debate. The future of work isn't either/or; it's both," said Brian Elliott of Future Forum. "A hybrid model can foster a more flexible and inclusive workplace, but only if leaders are intentional about establishing guardrails to ensure all employees have equal access to opportunity."[119]

The benefit of schedule flexibility results in better life balance, reduced stress, and more convenience for caregivers—women with children, in particular, are the ones who have the most affinity for schedule flexibility.

 People used to design their personal lives around work. Now they want to organize work around their personal lives. Flexibility is not only a vital indicator of happiness, it also enables your team to do great work.

In Step 5: Release Agility, I address why the new reality of work requires new norms and rules. To succeed in a hybrid workplace, you need a culture of freedom and accountability. Creating this culture requires getting rid of limiting rules and rethinking how decisions are made so teams can act faster and smarter.

DEFINE YOUR HYBRID WORK MODEL

Many companies say, "We are going hybrid," but it's not always clear what that means. "Hybrid" is a spectrum—from companies that require people to show up three specific days a week to those that shut down all but one office location. Defining your model is critical to succeeding in a hybrid workplace. Even more critical is including people in the process.

As I mentioned in Step 2, when the pandemic hit, the change management team at GoTo acknowledged that it was critical to empathize with employees. A series of company-wide interviews found six working personas that covered the whole spectrum—from working as a new hire to working while caring for adults.

Douglas Flory told me, "The personas landed really well when we shared them with employees. We created emojis for each and people started using them in Slack, creating empathy and great conversations about the specific challenges each group was facing."

This approach strengthened belonging and confirmed the importance of involving people in the journey. When GoTo went remote-first, the company used the personas to inform its decision and help employees adapt to the new model.

There are five basic types of hybrid and remote work models:

- Remote-friendly or office-first
- Fixed hybrid or buckets
- Partly remote or collaboration days
- Flexible hybrid or flexible schedule
- Remote-first or virtual-first

Each comes with its own pros and cons. In this chapter, we'll go over exactly what each one is and the implications of subscribing to a particular model.

5 TYPES OF HYBRID WORK MODELS

1. Remote-Friendly or "Office-First"

In an "office-first" model, there may be some flexibility around working remotely, but employees are still expected to spend most of their work time in the office. There are rules for which employees can work remotely on which days (usually one or two). Remote requests need to be approved by managers, and there is usually a structured approach that applies to everyone.

Remember Apple expecting everyone to work three days a week in the office? That's a perfect example of remote-friendly.

Remote-friendly is an improved version of the pre-pandemic workplace. However, it's a frustrating model that reflects the gap between what senior leaders want and what employees expect.

2. Fixed Hybrid or "Buckets"

The organization determines a set of categories in this scenario, and employees work according to the one they fall in. Leadership usually defines these buckets with little or no input from employees. For example, Citigroup categorized all jobs into three groups: resident, remote, or hybrid. In some roles, like branch-based or data centers, employees are expected to be fully in the office ("resident").[120]

The downside of this model is that it creates an unequal workplace. Some people have a lot of freedom and flexibility while others have none. Also, many assumptions behind the categories are based on how people *used* to work rather than exploring what the future could look like.

In contrast, HubSpot has also defined three buckets (@office, @flex, and @home) but allows employees to choose the one that works best for them. "Our hope is that by having a menu of options, employees can truly work when and where it's best for them."[121]

3. Partly Remote or "Collaboration Days"

In this setup, employees are expected to work on site the majority of the time but have the flexibility to work remotely a few days each week. Unlike the remote-friendly model, team members can choose the days they work remotely. As an example, Google decided that most employees would spend three "collaboration days" at the office and two days working from home.

The problem with this model is that it's still office-centric. Although it provides more flexibility to teams, it's based on the assumption that people need to be together to do great work. Most importantly, collaboration is structured around a schedule rather than a project or different modes of work.

4. Flexible Hybrid or Flexible Schedule

Employees can choose both their working hours and location in this model. It provides agency for teams to organize around work, integrating individual and collective preferences.

The biggest challenge of this model is that's less predictable. For example, it makes it harder to assess needs such as office space. It can also promote proximity bias. However, many of the tools we've discussed in previous chapters can help decrease these challenges while increasing belonging and participation. Moreover, teams can decide on when and why to get together based on the different collaboration modes.

Twitter has adopted this model and allows employees to work from home or the office, partially or full-time.

5. Remote-First or Virtual-First

In this model, remote work is the default mode for all employees. The company may retain office space for special occasions, such as events or design sprints, but all employees are expected to work remotely most of the time—and the leaders are, too.

Although it offers schedule flexibility, it's less flexible than a flexible hybrid model as working mostly from the office is not an option. This is a huge downside, especially for non-tech companies; forcing everyone to work entirely remotely can backfire. Also, some people prefer working from the office a majority of the time possibly because they lack a proper home office space or simply because of their personalities.

Dropbox adopted the "virtual-first" model while keeping offices in all their locations and hubs.[122] Their offices, now known as "studios," are collaborative and team-building spaces.

Implications

Flexible hybrid and remote-first models are the most ideal options as they address employee needs; they want to design their work schedule around their personal lives, not the other way around. Most importantly, it provides the autonomy, trust, and accountability needed to thrive in the new work reality. Many companies have hired new leaders for key roles who wouldn't have been available if they'd had to relocate.

Flexible hybrid and remote-first models provide a unique opportunity to rethink the workplace, improving the employee experience rather than going back to normal. Matt Mullenweg, CEO of Automattic said, "The primary mistake most companies make is to try to recreate the office online instead of taking advantage of what being fully digital allows you."

Mullenweg considers this workplace transformation a *moral imperative*: "Any company that can enable their people to be fully effective in a distributed fashion can and should do it far beyond after this current crisis has passed. But that doesn't mean it's going to be easy, or that the chaotic and stressful first taste some workplaces are getting right now is one that inspires them to keep trying."

In *Distributed Work's Five Levels of Autonomy*, Mullenweg encourages companies to move to Level Four—when things truly go asynchronous. "You evaluate people's work on what they produce, not how or when they produce it. Trust emerges as the glue that holds the entire operation together. You begin shifting to better—perhaps slower, but more deliberate—decision-making, and you empower everyone, not just the loudest or most extroverted, to weigh in on major conversations."[123]

The CEO hopes that companies could reach the ideal "nirvana" (Level Five): "When you consistently perform better than any in-person organization could... When people bring their best selves and highest levels of creativity to do the best work of their careers and just have fun."

 Hybrid is a spectrum in which you can continually evolve. Review the different models and select the one that works for you. Involve people along the journey. Define what hybrid really means to your organization.

As organizational psychologist Tasha Eurich told me: "Smart organizations openly talk about what it means to be a hybrid organization. They make it explicit, emphasizing the value of both remote and in-person collaboration."

Provide agency: Allow people to make choices about how and when to work. Eurich recommends, "As long as they are doing their work well, we should give our teams the opportunity to have the best of both worlds."

The following steps will help you develop the model best suited for your company:

1. Be clear. What does *hybrid* mean to your company? Choose your hybrid model wisely.
2. Decide how your approach will affect different areas. For example, manufacturing fully in-person, but legal and marketing flexible hybrid.
3. Clarify which arrangements will be made at the company level and how much flexibility teams and individuals will have.
4. Encourage your team to review the different work modes to design their workday around collaboration, not just schedules.
5. Review all your workflows. Will your existing ones work if you don't have 100% of the people at the office all the time? Design clear norms and rules that cover specific areas such as communication, hiring, or documentation (more on that later).
6. Revisit how decisions are made. A hybrid workplace requires distributing decision-making rights.
7. Monitor progress. Adapt your model and iterate based on what you learn from your different teams.
8. Make sure leaders model the right behavior.

Consider an example of how a company changed its rules. HubSpot's culture was built on the principle that power is gained by sharing knowledge, not hoarding it.

The marketing and sales software company doesn't have an "open-door" policy, it has a *no-door* policy.[124] Everyone has access to everyone in the organization.

When HubSpot became a publicly traded company, SEC regulations prohibited the company from continuing to share all information with employees. Chafing at the limitations imposed on its policy of full transparency, the company got around them by naming every employee an insider. At HubSpot, all information is once again open unless there is a legal requirement to keep it confidential or it's not owned by the company.

Remote work makes it imperative to explicitly define how each element of work occurs, being more intentional on communication, documentation, and collaboration. GitLab Head of Remote Darren Murph told me: "Leaders are much too focused on structuring informal conversation at the expense of not paying attention to structuring operations."

Making that shift is easier said than done. To thrive in a hybrid workplace, your team requires trust and freedom to choose how they want to work. Unfortunately, instead of curating their company culture, most leaders act as gatekeepers. In the next section, we'll discuss how their assumptions impede flexibility—and what you can do about it.

STEP 5: RELEASE AGILITY

TREAT PEOPLE THE WAY YOU WANT THEM TO BEHAVE—LIKE ADULTS

In many organizations, there is an unhealthy emphasis on process and not much freedom.
—Netflix Culture Memo

Too often, leaders' assumptions about employees, not actual performance, drive workplace rules. That's why most rules were created with offenders (3%) in mind but end up punishing the other 97% of employees as well.

Company rules should enable people, not limit them. The more autonomy allowed, the more accountable people will become. Freedom doesn't turn people into rogue employees—it makes them more responsible. If you want people to behave like adults, why treat them like children?

A few years ago, Netflix got rid of its traditional travel policy. It no longer told people how much money to spend, which airline class to book, or which hotel type to choose. The simplified "Act in Netflix's best interest" travel policy provides criteria—not instructions—allowing employees to make the best choice considering the context. Their good judgment has reduced Netflix's travel costs compared to when the company had a travel policy manual.[125]

Douglas McGregor, a midcentury professor of management at MIT, developed a philosophical view on what motivates people. His studies show that leaders' underlying assumptions about people generate two opposing theories.

"Theory X" is the assumption that people dislike work and put in the minimum effort. This approach presumes that people don't want to take responsibility and have little ambition. Thus, a command-and-control management style is the right response.

"Theory Y," on the other hand, presumes that people like to work as much as they like to play; it operates on the belief that people are self-directed. This approach assumes that everyone has potential, and that creativity, adaptation, and imagination are fairly distributed.[126]

Generally, organizations operate from negative assumptions. They adopt Theory X, thinking that people lack motivation.

Assumptions Leaders Make about People

THEORY X	THEORY Y
Dislike work. Find it boring.	Want to work. Can actually enjoy it.
People need supervision	People want independence
Motivated by fear and job security.	Motivated by purpose and self-development.
Just work for the money	Naturally want to work
People must be pushed to perform	People drive themselves to perform

Source: Douglas McGregor Theory X and Y

Author Daniel Pink believes there's a mismatch between what science knows and what business does; leaders are stuck in archaic views of what drives people. As I discussed in Step 2, Pink's research, shared in *Drive*, shows that companies still operate with what Pink calls "motivation 2.0," a carrot-and-stick approach that aligns with Theory X.

The problem with a reward and punishment system is that it generates short-term results. Most importantly, it encourages people to beat the system, not do their best work. "Rewards, by their very nature, narrow our focus," Pink said. "They concentrate the mind."

Motivation 3.0 is intrinsic—employees don't need to be managed by their boss to do their jobs. Autonomy, purpose, and mastery are what drive people.

Most CEOs love the principles of autonomy, but when it comes to pulling the trigger, they panic; they can't bring themselves trust that their employees will behave responsibly. In *Reinventing Organizations*, Frederic Laloux explains how this irrational belief is based on the unconscious assumptions that traditional hierarchies make about people.[127]

If you assume people are lazy, you won't give them more responsibility. If you believe they aren't trustworthy, you won't provide them with confidential information. The more you withhold, the more withdrawn people will become. The more withdrawn they become, the less engaged with work they'll be, and the less you're likely to trust them.

The assumptions organizations have about people are one of the great obstacles to creating a flexible workplace—one that requires freedom and accountability.

The solution is simple: start by examining your assumptions.

Do you believe people are good? Do you believe people add value? Or do you think they just want to make money? Are your assumptions based on perception or facts? What do your company rules say about your people?

Revisit rules and norms, both written and unwritten. See whether they are helping or limiting your team. Keep your rules simple and flexible, but don't forget to clarify expected behaviors and how performance will be measured.

Use this checklist to identify *limiting* rules:

- Rules that go against the team's/company's core values and purpose
- Rules that focus on negative behavior (what not do) versus promoting positive ones
- Rules that punish the majority of people instead of the few offenders
- Rules that treat people like children rather than adults
- Rules that slow down decision-making or hinder innovation

Replace limiting rules with a criterion that liberates people's ability to do great work—or maybe even get rid of them altogether. Capture the revised rules in the Hybrid Team Canvas. In the next chapter, we'll look at ways to adapt your pre-pandemic rules to the new world of work.

NEW WORLD, NEW NORMS

Are you still operating under rules that were created before the pandemic? The new reality of work requires a new approach. A thriving hybrid workplace requires flexibility and accountability.

Here are some ideas for adapting and recreating your rules.

Institute Flexible Scheduling

 Discuss what flexibility means when it comes to scheduling—must it be a company-wide approach or can team members design their own?

At Microsoft Europe, people can design their own work schedule. As Michel Bouman, EMEA Partner Technical Lead for Microsoft Teams Rooms, told me: "My workday starts at nine. My early morning is for my family. Then I stop at four p.m. to spend more time with my family and resume work in the evening. People enjoy being around their families more, to walk their children to school, have lunch together, or go for a walk."

Define Collaboration Time

App developer Project Imagine, named one of the best companies for remote workers, realized that the shift toward working from home required reconfiguring the workday.[128] Their redesigned remote workday defines a specific collaboration time: between ten a.m. and noon and between two p.m. and six p.m. All other times are out of bounds.

Establish a Response Frequency Protocol

In most teams, people are expected to respond to communications immediately. Little effort is made to protect one's ability to focus, and unclear expectations create unnecessary tensions.

Align your team on the expected response frequency per medium. What's an acceptable response time for an email? Or for Slack messages? Response time and frequency depends on the type of work and the roles each member play—customer service, for example, needs to be more responsive than other departments.

It also helps to have a line on your email signature that clarifies how often you check your email. Not only does this reminds team members of the agreement, it also sets expectations for people outside the organization who are not familiar with your rules.

Create a Plan for Emergencies

It is useful to know how to reach someone in an emergency. An escalation rule can help identify who should be contacted and which specific channel or method to use. This helps people understand that, if the protocol has been activated, it is a real emergency.

If there's an emergency at Slack's Future Forum team that requires contacting someone outside of office hours, team members are required to send a text message to that person's personal phone. They will never send a Slack message at seven p.m. if something is urgent. People are not supposed to check or respond to messages in Slack after regular working hours.

Encourage People to Take Time Off

Even when organizations adopt a Netflix-like unlimited vacation policy, it often happens that their workplace culture is not ready and people simply don't take time off.

That's something Adobe realized—despite feeling burned out, most employees weren't taking time off. Travel restrictions due to the pandemic weren't helping, so people put off their vacation days. Focus groups showed that employees could benefit from the entire company taking a break simultaneously. In response, Adobe instituted a global day off one Friday per month.[129]

Assume Good Intent

Misunderstandings can happen more often in a hybrid workplace. If we're not careful, issues can get blown out of proportion because we assume rather than try to understand what the other person meant.

Help Scout, a provider of helpdesk software, encourages employees to "assume miscommunication over malice." This principle protects people from feeling attacked by others. The notion is shared with new hires on their first day.

This principle is particularly important to teams and companies with a diverse set of employees. Creating a culture that assumes good intent can go a long way toward smoothing over cultural misunderstandings.

Summarize More, Chat Less

Constant pings and messages are a distraction leading to more reactive, less thoughtful communication. Even worse, lots of tiny pieces of information spread out over time or channels tend to create confusion and misunderstanding. It's just hard to put it all together.

Instead, substitute constant chatting with summaries. At Just Eat Takeaway, a food delivery app, the team lead shares a "top of mind" document. It includes a collection of the key topics she wants to discuss. If something new comes up, she adds it to the next week's document.

Assume Low Context

Be considerate of the people you are communicating with. Don't assume they have all the background information you have or that they can read your mind. Provide some context so the recipient can understand where you are coming from.

If you have a request, be specific about:

- When you need it (a specific time, whether it's urgent, etc.)
- Why you are asking for something
- Action required: "Feedback needed," "Approval Required," "FYI," or "No response needed"

Before hitting "send," ask yourself: Is it clear? Will the other person understand what I need? Am I providing enough context?

Make a Slack Agreement

Messaging tools are powerful for remote teams. However, the lack of a clear protocol can turn them into a nightmare, bringing the worst of synchronous and asynchronous communication together.

Ula Iwanska, head of talent & culture at Awell Health, kindly shared its Slack agreement in one of my training programs:

Slack is great for:

- Social conversations, interesting links, chit-chat
- Urgent questions and requests that need a quick response
- Real-time conversation with people who are available on Slack
- Conversations that can be had asynchronously
- Sharing need-to-knows and FYIs
- Celebrations and praise
- Sharing interesting read/link
- Monitoring and logging (through third-party software)

Avoid Slack for:

- Discussions that require a lot of context
- Making major decisions (create a decision page)
- Sharing ways of working/processes
- Giving in-depth feedback—do in a private meeting

Pay for the Role, Not the Location

Compensation for remote employees is controversial. Many companies such as Facebook and Google have adopted location-based compensation policies, meaning that if an employee relocates away from their offices in the expensive San Francisco Bay Area, their salary will be adjusted.

The principle is flawed. Not only were these companies very profitable while paying those salaries, they are now saving overhead costs as people work remotely. Most importantly, the value employees provide is the same—so why penalize them?

When Spotify announced its Work from Anywhere approach, the company stated it would continue to pay at San Francisco or New York salary rates, based on the type of job.[130] That's in stark contrast to other tech companies.

Real estate website Zillow has moved away from a location-based approach. Chief people officer Dan Spaulding said, "Your long-term earning potential is determined by how you perform, and will not be limited by where you live." He went on to say that this stand will help Zillow attract and retain the best talent.

Define Workspace Setup

Technology and workplace equipment are crucial for providing remote workers with a good employee experience. Yet, many employees are underwhelmed by their current technology experience. Research by Microsoft shows that 42% of employees say they lack essential office supplies at home, and 10% don't have an adequate internet connection to do their job.[131]

Establish the approach and budget your company will provide based on your hybrid work model. Offer options that consider the realities of the different groups.

HubSpot offers different arrangements for each of their three buckets:

- @office employees have a dedicated desk for their laptop, monitor, family photos, and anything else they want. They can take the laptop home but don't have an at-home desk setup.
- @flex employees are allocated a "hotel desk," organized by the team when they come to the office. HubSpot supports their work-from-home setup.
- @home employees' WFH setup is ensured by HubSpot to be safe and sound.

Let People Know "We've Got You"

Broadcasting to your colleagues that you need to take time off should be sufficient. In a high-trust culture, employees shouldn't have to explain what's going on in their personal lives unless they want to.

At Forma, a benefit service app, caring for others and supporting each other is a priority for all. "We've got you" is one of their four values (Disclaimer: I helped them revise and update their values). Forma employees are expected to ask for help and advice when needed. If they're going through a hard time, they just let others know and take a break. "We've got you covered."

Work Handbook-First

Documentation is the foundation of successful remote teams, building more robust, informed, trusting, and connected collaboration. When you're working from home, you don't have the luxury of visiting someone's desk to ask a question or joining in a conversation. Documentation is an efficient way to find answers without needing human help.

GitLab recommends a handbook-first approach.[132] Employees embrace a "pay-it-forward" mentality; by helping new employees get all the answers, they train them to help others.

Making documentation everyone's responsibility ensures inclusion and avoids the burden of having only a few people take care of it.

Revamp Recruitment

The remote interview has its challenges but also opens possibilities to do things differently. Why replicate the boring, old-fashioned interview process when you can turn it into an experience?

Twitter uses pair interviewing exclusively. One person takes the lead in conducting the interview, while the other observes more closely and takes notes. Pair interviewing provides a different perspective.

At Liberty IT in Ireland, they use a similar approach, having the candidate solve a coding problem with two team members. The practice goes beyond understanding how good people are at problem-solving. It sheds light on questions such as: Do they ask great questions? Are they good collaborators?

Hire for Remote Culture Fitness

Hiring people with remote-first experience will help build a digital-first culture. People who are good communicators, autonomous, and obsessive about documentation are vital to strengthening your skills.

Automattic, a fully remote company of several hundred employees, interviews developers over text-based chat only.[133] This helps identify candidates who are good communicators—they are clear, use the right tone, and are to the point—while also helping to reduce bias in the hiring process. "We are definitely a writing-first company," Mullenweg told me. "Whether that's influenced me or whether I influenced it, it's probably been too long to tell."

He also says clear writing is something that Automattic looks for in new candidates: "It doesn't have to be fancy writing or anything like that. In fact, for half of our company, English is not their first language. It's important that they took the time to make sure that the most important points are the most important things in the text."

Decentralize Culture-Building

In a hybrid workplace, work no longer is office-centric. Your culture shouldn't be, either.

When GoTo went fully remote, the company decided to pivot. With the money saved on office space, it started funding a community program. The company geo-mapped where employees lived and assigned a local leader, and corresponding budget, per area. Each local "chapter" can run local team rituals and volunteering events to support local communities.

Prepare for Interruptions

No matter how organized your team is, you will never get rid of all interruptions. What if, instead of trying to eliminate them, you prepare your team to better deal with them?

Here are some recommendations RescueTime offered after interviewing its users:

Awareness. Simply bringing up the issue of interruptions helps coworkers be more mindful of how often they drop by or send messages.

Schedule interruptions. Create "interruption-free" times in the day, like office hours or lunch breaks. Check if people are free before interrupting them.

Rethink the way you communicate. Establish response protocols that help minimize interruptions.[134]

SPEED IS A COMPETITIVE ADVANTAGE

Moving fast is critical to accelerating performance, especially in times of disruption. Speed is a competitive advantage. It helps organizations outperform their competitors in terms of profitability, operational resilience, and business growth.

But what makes or breaks organizational speed? Decision-making.

You can't have effective leadership without effective decisions. However, most organizations struggle with decision-making. A study by McKinsey showed that only 28% of executives praised the quality of their company's decisions; the majority believed that bad decisions were as frequent as good ones.[135] Decision-making problems become even more pronounced in a hybrid situation because distance tends to magnify existing issues.

In one of his famous letter to shareholders, Jeff Bezos explained how Amazon deals with this challenge: " Our senior team is determined to keep our decision-making velocity high. Speed matters in business—plus a high-velocity decision-making environment is more fun too."[136]

Amazon's founder acknowledged that his team doesn't have all the answers—decision-making is not a perfect process. Smaller companies have less to lose; that's why they move faster. Bezos recommends integrating the scope and capabilities of a large company with the spirit and heart of a small one.

Decidophobia is the fear of making decisions, leading to analysis paralysis. Leaders want to avoid the cost of making the wrong call. However, inaction is not a risk-free choice; it can be more harmful than making an imperfect decision. Always consider the cost of inaction: "What's the impact of *not* making this decision?"

 Most companies lack clarity and alignment on how decisions should be made. Moreover, they don't acknowledge that making decisions isn't just the responsibility of managers. People need the skills and authority to make calls about the work they are doing. Front line employees and those closest to the problem are usually better equipped to make decisions.

Perfectionism is a crucial barrier, but not the only one. Trying to anticipate every possible scenario and making sure all risks are resolved can bog your team down. The risks of inaction are greater than the risks of decisive action. Acting quickly will give your company an edge.

Making decisions remotely adds some extra challenges. If your team works in different time zones, it becomes harder to involve everyone. Similarly, when not everyone is in the same (virtual) room, some opinions might be left out. Lack of clear communication channels is also an issue. Making decisions in a hybrid team requires using asynchronous communication to include everyone.

Following are some things to keep in mind as you decide how to decide.

Authorize People to Make Decisions

Decentralizing decision-making increases speed and also helps people make better decisions. Most decisions are reversible and changeable. Amazon calls these everyday, operational decisions "Type 2" decisions. As a rule of thumb, those who are closer to the issue or have more information should be able to make the call, but they need the formal authority to make those decisions. Distribute decision-making rights so people can manage Type 2 decisions without asking for permission.

Type 1 decisions, on the other hand, are more complex/high-risk and should be made slowly and methodically, with more consultation and deliberation.

Move Faster with Safe-to-Try Decisions

There's no such thing as a perfect decision. The right decision made at the wrong time isn't any better than a wrong decision. Speed and timing are everything. Adopting "safe-to-try" decisions will help you move forward rather than wait for the perfect solution. When feeling stuck, ask: "Will the decision move the team backward or cause harm that cannot be mitigated promptly?"

This litmus test helps validate a proposal by addressing every team member's objections. Smart organizations adopt an agile, test-and-learn mindset when making decisions. Virgin's Richard Branson said, "In business, if you realize you've made a bad decision, you change it." That's the spirit behind safe-to-try decisions. You can always course correct.

Integrate Emotion, Intuition, and Rationality

Are you data-driven or data-informed? The difference isn't just semantic. Data-driven means letting data guide your decisions. Data-informed is using data as one basis for decision-making, but not the only one.

The point is not to dismiss the value of data but to integrate other elements, too. According to research by the Harvard Business Review, "experience and knowledge of leaders in the subject matter still outperform purely data-driven approaches."[137]

Feelings lubricate, rather than impair, rationality, said neuroscientist Antonio Damasio.[138] Feelings not only help us make choices but are a critical part of human reasoning.

Companies Buurtzorg, Morningstar, and AES use multiple sources to inform their decision-making processes:

- Rationality: Rational, analytical approaches are critical, but not the only factor.
- Emotions: Recognize the power of inquiry, "Why am I angry, fearful, ambitious, or excited? What does this reveal about me or about the situation that is unfolding?"
- Intuition: Reality is usually ambiguous, paradoxical, and nonlinear. Intuition uncovers wisdom in surprising ways, unconsciously connecting the dots.

Commit (Even If You Disagree)

Even the soundest decision will fail if it's not supported. Full commitment is required for success. Disagreement is helpful, but at some point, will people gamble with you on it? Will they commit even if they initially resisted the decision? No one can predict the outcome of a decision with certainty. However, when everyone commits, the odds are on your side.

Atlassian applies the "disagree and commit" principle. It's usually too difficult or too slow to get the entire team feeling wonderful about a decision, but once the call is made, everyone should commit to supporting it. As Atlassian's former product manager Matt Russell explained: "It's healthy to disagree, offer up your perspective, and support it with data. But at the end of the day, we agree to rally around the decision and work to make it successful, regardless of whether we prefer it or not."

Don't Worry about What You Don't Know

As human beings, we can't deal with uncertainty, thus we try to control even what's out of our hands. By worrying about what we don't know, we get stuck in fear and endless analysis.

Instead, ask "What should we do, given that we have imperfect information?"

Jeff Bezos believes that most decisions should probably be made with around 70% of the information we wish we had. Waiting for more will slow us down. Moving fast is not about answering every possible question or eliminating all risks, but making the right choice with *imperfect* information. You can always course correct. Act based on what you know— you'll figure the other 30% out along the way, once you're implementing the decision.

"HOW DOES YOUR TEAM MAKE DECISIONS?"

I often ask this question when I start working with a new client. I have team members write down their responses individually. When we consolidate the notes, the answers usually don't match. Everyone has a different perception of how decisions are (or should be) made.

How can a team make good decisions when they are not even aligned on the decision-making process? To move fast, it's imperative that your remote team explicitly defines who will decide and, most importantly, how.

Having a shared decision-making approach not only brings clarity but also increases performance. It's an invitation to reflect on the different types of decisions your team makes, the different decision-making methods, and how to reconcile both.

There are seven essential decision-making methods:

- Autocratic
- Delegation
- Democratic
- Consent
- Avoidance
- Consultative
- Consensus

Let's review the characteristics of each and when to use them.

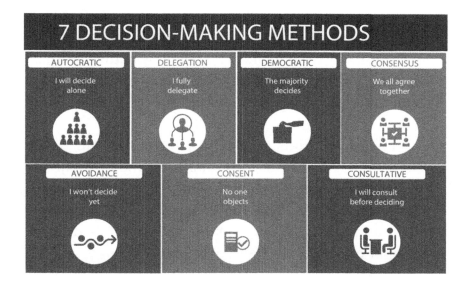

The **Autocratic** method is when one person holds full authority to decide without needing input or approval from others. It works well for decisions that need to happen fast. For example, Zappos delegates full authority to its customer representatives, allowing them to decide the best way to solve a client's issue without having to consult their managers.

You can also assign a "directly responsible individual" (DRI), a term coined by Apple to refer to the one person with whom the buck stops on any given project.[139] A DRI is ultimately held accountable for the success (or failure) of that project.

Delegation is when someone who holds the authority to make a decision transfers it temporarily to someone else. This can help untangle issues when someone is too busy or too distant from the issue to handle it appropriately, like when a manager takes a vacation and delegates specific responsibilities to team members. Delegation transfers temporary authority to someone who might be better informed to decide, and it's a good opportunity to train people to make decisions.

Democratic methods give power to the people. Team members discuss options, call for a vote, and the majority wins. It's important to clarify what the majority is. For some companies, it can be anything above 50%; others request a majority of over 70% to move forward. Also, you might consider a weighted system. At Hugo, a meeting software company, the person ultimately responsible for the work or decision gets triple voting power, those affected by the decision have double power, and the rest, only single power.

Consensus means that everyone must agree to the decision before the team can move forward. This method not only involves everybody but requests everyone's permission to do something. Unlike the Democratic method, the team cannot move forward if even one person disagrees. This method slows down decision-making, is subject to compromises, and is hard to implement in large groups.

The **Consultative** method is when someone making a decision invites input from others but ultimately makes, and is responsible for, the decision. At Netflix, captains are in charge of large projects and have full authority to make the call, but need to get input from others to decide.

Be clear about why you are asking for input; some people confuse being consulted with a Democratic method, but there's a difference between providing input and voting.

Consent addresses objections from team members until there's an agreement to accept a good-enough solution. Consent is not the same as Consensus; it means that no one opposes the idea even if they don't agree. A variation of the Consultative method, it includes a series of well-defined steps in which the proposer shares the recommended solution, colleagues ask clarifying questions and react to the proposal, and objections are discussed. If all objections are resolved, the proposal moves forward. If not, it might need to be amended or canceled.

Avoidance is when a decision is put on the back burner until the right time or more information arrives. It can be detrimental when a decision is urgent. However, when used intentionally, delaying a decision can be beneficial in the long run. This method works well when there's a lot of ambiguity or when postponing a decision won't create a negative consequence. Sometimes, the best decision is not to make one.

Decide how your team makes decisions and capture them in the Hybrid Team Canvas.

Context Is Everything

No decision method is perfect; they all have pros and cons. The nature, context, and types of particular decisions might require different methods. Consider whether the decision is urgent or requires participation from others. As a rule of thumb, when a decision will impact people's work or them personally, you should get their input.

The chart below shows where these decision-making methods fall on the continuums of not urgent to urgent and individual to collective.

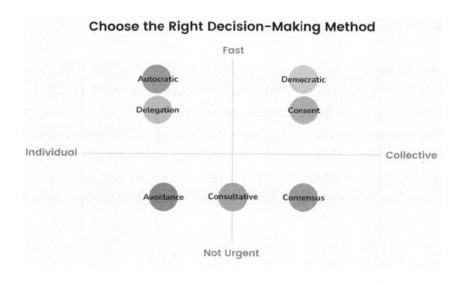

A Democratic approach is good for making simple choices, like choosing a time or day to meet. However, it can lower the bar when used to select ideas. Gathering consensus is a more prolonged process than making autocratic decisions.

Still, it might be effective for very sensitive topics (a team hiring a candidate) or in small groups (an executive team deciding on an acquisition). A Consultative approach works perfectly when the decision will impact others or when its complexity requires input from diverse experts.

The context could affect your approach. Many companies have a dual decision-making process, as Airbnb does. In regular times, employees have full authority, but they must first consult data scientists to inform their decisions. Airbnb's managers are just facilitators; employees make final decisions. However, during a crisis, there's no room for consensus or participation.

Brian Chesky learned from experience that he needs to act fast when the company faces a crisis. In 2011, he failed to do so after a female host's apartment was destroyed and her identity stolen by a renter. A media firestorm followed. Chesky got involved and apologized. "We should have responded faster, communicated more sensitively, and taken more decisive action to make sure she felt safe and secure."[140] Since then, Airbnb's CEO takes over when a crisis hits the company.

Teams should have more than one decision method, taking into account the context that affects the impact: urgent versus not urgent, crisis situations versus normal ones, minimal versus substantial implications, etc.

Create a Decision-Making Page

We have already discussed how documenting everything is critical to make your hybrid team more effective and avoid miscommunication. The same applies to decisions. Having a decision-making page will help your team align on how to make decisions and stay informed.

The Belgian health care technology start-up Awell Health has made 40 key decisions in just four months since it implemented the "decision page" method. Ula Iwanska said, "This approach, though time-consuming, yields the most thoughtful decisions in a very short amount of time. The bonus is well-documented decisions available for everyone to see."

Not every decision needs a decision page; only high-impact ones do. Here are some tips for creating yours:

- Capture each key decision in a document. It's a slow process, but time invested is time saved; you will avoid mistakes, miscommunication, and interruptions because employees can always refer to the decisions page.

- Provide context: People must understand why a decision was made. Most importantly, if the context changes, the team can propose new solutions. It makes it easier to bring new team members up to speed.

- Use the following questions to capture the context:

  - What information was available at the time?
  - What were the decision-making steps?
  - Why was the decision made?

- Use a written document to get input. When using a Consultative approach, it's more efficient to make comments on a document. Everyone can build on others' input, too.

- Encourage people to vote asynchronously. A document is time-agnostic. If you are using Consensus or Democratic methods, people can vote on their own time within a set deadline.

- Provide time to reflect. Asynchronous communication helps make better decisions, decision strategist Annie Duke explains in her book, *How to Decide*.[141] It helps avoid biases, makes us more considerate of others' perspectives, and encourages us to be fairer with ourselves and others.

- Keep it alive. A decision-making document should not only help track what happened but also evolve your team's decisions. Having important decisions well-documented makes them accessible to everyone in the company and can provide input to improve a decision.

WHAT SUCCESSFUL REMOTE LEADERS DO DIFFERENTLY

Releasing agility not only requires revisiting norms, rules, and decision-making but also our unhealthy relationship with leadership. For decades, we were taught to see leaders as heroes, here to save the day. From movies and management books to internet quotes and TED Talks, we've been spoon-fed a glamorized view of what being a leader really is.

As Hortense le Gentil wrote about this in *Harvard Business Review.* "These leaders appeared to be born hero leaders, naturally endowed with supreme intelligence, coming up with brilliant ideas and directives from the mountaintop that lower echelons were then expected to execute. The pandemic has highlighted what was already becoming clear before the emergence of the virus: that hero leaders are no longer what companies need."[142]

 The truth is, we don't need heroic leaders. We need human beings who take care of people.

The traits traditionally valued in leaders—confidence, charisma, and extroversion—don't translate into virtual leadership. Research shows that people prefer leaders who take care of people and culture, foster interpersonal connections, provide help and resources, and most importantly, get things done—basically, leaders who are dependable, productive, and helpful.[143]

"The role of leaders is to take care of people, not to pass orders or be the hero," le Gentil told me. "Leaders need to stop trying to be the fixer. Instead of being the ones who solve all the problems, leaders need to become better at listening, paying attention, and being fully present. Sometimes, people need time and support, not a solution."

So, what does it take to shift from hero to human?

1. Trust More—Even If It's Not Comfortable

For most leaders, the trust battery starts at around 50% when a new colleague joins the team. To increase that trust level, new members must prove that they are trustworthy through their behavior.

The problem is that 50% is not enough. Trust is a two-way street. Leaders must take the first step and supercharge their own trust battery. Working in a hybrid environment requires trusting employees more than ever, and leaders must learn to trust their team more than feels comfortable.

Doist CMO Brenna Loury wrote, "The most important lesson you can imbue in a new team member is that trust is assumed, not earned." She suggests a list of gestures that managers can make to help the new person feel trusted from day one.

- Simply be available
- Communicate honestly and frequently

- Assign meaningful work to new members
- Clearly define expectations from day one
- Encourage people to get to know each other

2. Take Care of the Culture, Not the Work

As a leader, you can't be both a player and a coach. Trying to be both is bound to fail. Borrow some inspiration from sports coaches. Their role is to build a strong team and a winning culture; they don't play the match.

Great remote leaders focus on building the right environment. They take care of the culture, not the work, and trust that their people will do what it takes to get the job done. Team coach Emily Bond suggested: "I would get back to basics and encourage the leader to revisit norms and agreements as a team. How might norms need to evolve to better suit hybrid? Has each team member shared what's working and what isn't? What is the team committed to changing?"

Take care of the culture so your team can focus on the game.

3. Walk a Mile in Your Employees' Shoes

As a manager, you are responsible for leading your team during your workplace transformation and for modeling new collaboration practices. You must be intentional about creating an equitable experience for every employee, including equal access to leaders, career opportunities, learning and development, and belonging.

Start by getting out of the office and into the remote experience so you can empathize with your employees—and make sure it's the full experience, not just a token. Try working from your kitchen table, with low-speed internet, no extra child care, and no delivered lunch.

John Chappel, portfolio manager at Capita Software, suggests: "Try working remotely yourself, not just for one day, but at least three, ideally five. It will give you a feel for the challenges and the benefits."

4. Embrace the Unknown

Many leaders struggle with the hybrid workplace because they are scared of losing control. They're afraid of being vulnerable and admitting that they don't know what it takes to effectively lead a remote team.

It's okay to feel lost and unsure about how to do remote right. When Torben Friehe and Yann Leretaille started Wingback as an all-remote company, they were lost, too. But the cofounders were brave enough to acknowledge their fears.

Moshe Mikanovsky, senior product manager at Procom Labs, the tech arm of a talent acquisition company, says getting it right will require experimentation and iteration. "Try and adjust. Don't plan it all up-front to death! It will work differently for you than it will for other companies. Do it in baby steps. See what works and what doesn't."

Sometimes, you have to get it wrong before you can get it right.

5. Design Opportunities for Serendipity

Casual collaboration includes incidental and impromptu interactions with colleagues. It strengthens social bonds and shared values that enable trust and teamwork. As discussed in Step 4, casual collaboration is the foundation of substantial social capital, building the base for deep collaboration.

Intentionally design opportunities for serendipity with an end goal in mind. Even in the office, impromptu encounters don't happen entirely by chance.

Marissa Goldberg, founder of Remote Work Prep, explained there are two big parts to serendipity: structure and permission. "Structure in the office [meant] you have to be there at the specific time, at the specific building, and that's how you run into each other. Second, there was permission. Your employer made you feel safe enough to get up from your desk and grab a coffee and not be seen as a slacker."

Leaders should deliberately create the structure and permission necessary for casual interactions to take place. Review previous sections of the book for inspiration.

6. Model Asynchronous Behavior

Transitioning to asynchronous-first collaboration requires demonstrating the right mindsets and behaviors. What you do is as important as what you say. Once your team defines new norms and ways of collaborating, people will look to you to see if the change is for real.

Block time for focus work and invite others to do the same. Respect your own and others' calendars. Avoid responding to emails or Slack messages immediately—respect the agreements. Use and respect away messages, whether it's a "busy" status on Slack or an "out of the office" auto-respond email. Be mindful of time zone differences.

Brian Elliot of Future Forum set up a standard with his team regarding Slack notification. He only reads the messages directed to him or when he's @ mentioned in a channel. This creates clear expectations about how he will respond and encourages his team to do the same.

Recap

STEP 5: RELEASE AGILITY

A successful hybrid workplace requires a culture of freedom and accountability.

Define the hybrid model that works best for your company's needs but remember that the more flexibility, the better.

Company rules should enable people, not limit them.

Enabling swift decisions is a competitive advantage requiring authority distribution across the team.

The role of remote leaders is to take care of people and culture, facilitating conversations around what the culture *is* and what it *should be*.

YOUR TURN:
LEADING A HYBRID TEAM

Now that we've covered the roadmap to designing a hybrid workplace culture, let's see how we can bring all the pieces together so you can make the critical decisions necessary to act.

Start working on this activity whether or not you have completed each of the earlier exercises. To complete this one, however, you'll have to revisit the ideas and tools in the book.

The Leading in a Hybrid Workplace Canvas covers four areas crucial for thriving in a hybrid workplace: Define, Design, Demonstrate, and Demand.

Define is choosing the right hybrid model for your company or team.

Design is intentionally designing the different building blocks of culture.

Demonstrate is modeling the right behaviors to align words with action.

Demand is setting clear expectations for team members.

Although some of the areas are primarily the leaders'
responsibility, team members must be consulted and
should actively contribute along the journey. We'll cover
them one by one in the order you need to complete
them. As soon as you finish one part, you can start
working on the next.

The infinity sign in the canvas is a reminder that culture
design is a never-ending process. You need to revisit it
and iterate.

LEADING IN A HYBRID WORKPLACE
Define, Design, Demonstrate, and Demand Your Hybrid Culture

Team name _____   Date _____

Design   Demand

Define   Demonstrate

Designed by Gustavo Razzetti
FearlessCulture

www.fearlessculture.design

Fearless Culture

Scan this QR code to download your copy.

Define

Define your remote work model and culture, ensuring that it's clear to everybody and supported by all. Your company probably has a policy that was defined earlier in the pandemic. Now that things are starting to settle, it's time to revisit it. I strongly advise against calling it a "back-to-the-office" policy because that misses the point. This is an opportunity to think differently.

Establish your hybrid work model

Revisit the five hybrid work models we covered earlier. Evaluate the pros and cons and discuss them with your team. Reflect on the pains and gains for both the company and the team members. It's critical to get input, not just buy-in.

Take into account the different characteristics of your organization. Should the model apply across all departments, or do you need to customize it to certain areas?

This is a time to explore possibilities. Put aside assumptions like "all customer service reps should be in the office every day." Invite your team to come up with alternatives. The goal is not to please everyone but to avoid repeating past patterns; seize the opportunity to reinvent your organization.

Craft your hybrid work policy

Don't just state your policy. Explain why you created it and what problems it's trying to solve. Are there options that will require eligibility or that are limited to certain functions? Will people need to request permission from their managers? How will the policy affect salaries? Will the company cover tech and home office costs?

Clarify levels of flexibility

How much room do team members have to make personal choices? Ideally, you are adopting a flexible work schedule. In that case, will the definition of "flexible" be decided by a manager, team, or department?

Consider defining collaboration hours in which people must be available for meetings, calls, etc., and also blocking out protected time for people to do deep work. Flexibility should be the main driver, but try to balance individual needs with group expectations.

The more flexible the model, the more complex it becomes—at first. However, don't let short-term needs or comfort guide your decision-making. Choose what's best for the long run, even if it requires initial extra effort. It will pay off over time.

Design

In this part, assess, review, and design the different building blocks of culture:

- Values
- Behavior You Reward and Punish
- Purpose
- Priorities
- Feedback
- Rituals
- Psychological Safety
- Meetings
- Decision-Making
- Norms & Rules

Assess your current culture, reviewing each of the key building blocks:

- What's working?
- What's not working?
- What's missing?

Get your team together and cover each of the building blocks, one at a time. After the assessment, revisit the respective steps and look for tools or exercises to help you tackle what's not working or what's missing.

Capture the decisions in the Hybrid Team Canvas introduced in Step 4—create one source of truth or team agreement.

Demonstrate

Leaders' actions speak louder than words. Ensure that your behavior—your decisions, what you reward, priorities, and how you show up—align with the defined culture.

Be human

People don't need heroes. They need human, vulnerable, empathetic, helpful, and emotionally intelligent leaders. How will you model vulnerability and be supportive and helpful?

Practice intellectual humility by leading with questions, not answers.

Be consistent

Leadership results from what we do repeatedly. Your collective behavior, not just isolated actions, shapes culture. How are you going to hold yourself account-able? Invite your team to call you out when they see your behavior is inconsistent with the desired culture.

Be transparent

Transparency is not about sharing everything but about not hiding what people need to know. How will you share information with your team and keep them up to speed?

Be candid, but care about the person both when sharing feedback as well as bad news.

Be respectful

Treat people with respect, not just as professionals but as human beings. How will you respect their personal time or decisions?

Show respect to the person, their intentions, and their work.

Be flexible

Embrace an experimental mindset; be ready to fail and adjust your course. How will you deal with mistakes? How will you react to uncertainty and criticism?

Promote a flexible mindset by sharing your mistakes and asking for help when needed.

Demand

Clarify expectations so that people understand how they need to contribute. Most importantly, define what's okay and what's not. Be specific and invite your team to reflect and identify their individual commitment to moving the team in the right direction.

Consider things like availability, responsiveness to emails and pings, when to be open for collaboration, which tech tools to use for what, and other team agreements.

Use the Start, Stop, Continue construct to clarify expectations:

Start

What do we need to start doing differently? What practices or workflows do we need to adopt moving forward? What behaviors, mindsets, or activities do we need to begin implementing in the next cycle?

Consider both places for improvement and areas for experimentation.

Examples:

- Start asking more questions of our leader rather than assume we understood their vision.

- Start addressing conflict earlier, before it becomes unmanageable.
- Start protecting focus/deep work time.
- Start trusting new hires from day one.

Stop

What are things that no longer serve us? What behaviors and practices harm us, which do we need to let go?

Examples:

- Stop scheduling meetings for conversations that can happen asynchronously.
- Stop working on initiatives that are not aligned with our team's priorities.
- Stop starting "the next big thing" before finishing projects that move the needle.
- Stop trying to solve urgent issues via Slack.

Continue

What behaviors, mindsets, or activities should stay as part of the team's best practices?

Examples:

- Continue helping each other and sharing resources across projects.
- Continue check-in rounds to see how our colleagues are doing.

- Continue reflecting on how we align our decisions with our purpose.
- Continue providing context when requesting people to do something.

You can use the Start, Stop, Continue exercise to reflect on team performance, the business as a whole, or a particular project.

Capture the conclusions and agreements on the canvas. Revisit it monthly and focus on areas that need to be improved or changed. I can't repeat this enough: Designing your hybrid work culture is a never-ending job.

Enjoy the journey.

Afterword

THE CULTURE THAT WILL GET YOU THERE

Every book must end.

Writing *Remote, Not Distant* was a transformational journey.
I started with many hypotheses. Some were confirmed, many
were discarded, and others evolved. I had some initial thoughts
on where to take the book but didn't know I would land here.

As I interviewed people, collecting stories of how organizations have adapted to the changing workplace, I observed
both pain and excitement. I met leaders who are still lost and
trying to recover a sense of normalcy. And I met many who
were brave enough to admit they didn't have the answers
and are figuring things out together with their teams.

I talked to people who would rather lose their jobs than the freedom and flexibility they gained during the pandemic. I met advocates of remote work who think that having an office is pointless. And, of course, I encountered skeptics. Not everyone is willing to accept that "the way we've always done things" no longer serves them.

In the introduction, I shared the backlash Apple faced after expecting employees to return to the office. What has changed since then? A lot—and yet, not much. As I'm writing this afterword, Google announced that its voluntary work-from-home model is over. As I mentioned in Step 5, it has adopted a hybrid approach that will require people to work three "collaboration days" at the office going forward.

The move has sparked a massive reaction in social media and beyond.[144] Many skeptics are calling Google's decision "a step backward." Experts believe it lacks empathy as many employees have relocated or have conflicts in their personal lives. The push to return to the office feels like a missed opportunity, from reducing Google's carbon footprint to providing the flexibility people crave for. Some think the tech giant will lose key talent.

To be honest, though, not all of Google's employees are complaining. Some want to return to the office. Others have been granted permission to work fully remotely and are excited to have a "home base" for whenever they want to go into the office.

So, what's driving Google's choice? The same reason that forced the WFH revolution: the pandemic. Only now that COVID-19 is seemingly under control, the company believes it's the right time to come back because of "advances in prevention and treatment, the steady decline in cases [...], and the improved safety measures," as John Casey, Google's vice president of global benefits, wrote in an email to employees.

But a safer environment simply isn't enough to justify returning to the office. Google is missing an opportunity to leverage everything it's learned from working remotely. The culture that got you here won't get you into the future.

Google's decision makes sense if you consider its history. The company has invested millions in creating some of the most quirky, beautifully designed, and creative offices, which come with perks like free gourmet meals, bikes, in-house massage rooms, and fabulous parties. Google fears that culture can be harmed because employees are missing this experience.

However, as I argue in this book, those elements are *part* of the culture, but not *the* culture. Creating a strong workplace culture is not office-dependent. As Automattic CEO Matt Mullenweg told me, "What changed is that before, a lot of people thought that remote work wasn't possible and now have experienced how great it can be. I guess it's not the people making those decisions, but probably their bosses for whom the office was probably a lot nicer than for the rest. Ultimately, the power lies in people, especially in tech companies because it's a very competitive market."

 The biggest mistake companies make is defining their hybrid work model based on the pains, not the gains, of remote work.

Most gains, like less commuting, more flexibility, and convenience, are employee-based. But there are also many wins for the company, including happier employees and fewer overhead costs. Unfortunately, leaders tend to make decisions mostly based on the pains. They define their model to solve for (potential) issues such as lack of control, erosion of culture, a shared identity, a well-designed office experience, to name a few.

Your workplace culture is a collection of choices.

As you digest all the stories, insights, tools, and activities I've covered in this book, make sure your decisions consider gains as well as pains.

Include people in the process. Understand their expectations and needs, inviting them to come up with new ideas and solutions. Most importantly, remember that the more agency you give people, the more accountable they become.

Whatever model you end up choosing, keep one thing in mind: don't erase all the progress made when your team was forced to work from home. Avoid the temptation to go back to normal simply for its own sake.

Thriving in a hybrid workplace requires thoughtfulness and intentionality. Check-in rounds, regular one-on-ones, peer-to-peer feedback, and leveling the playing field in meetings, to name a few, can help teams work better. Build on your own playbook and experiment with the multiple tools I've shared here.

Reset your culture. Reimage a shared future with your team. Reignite a sense of belonging, being more intentional about psychological safety, feedback, and rituals. Rethink the notion of collaboration, defaulting to asynchronous mode. Release agility. Choose the hybrid model that best works for your organization, eliminating limiting rules and distributing decision-making authority.

Writing a book is a never-ending journey. The same is true of the hybrid workplace. Be ready to experiment and iterate. This book is finished, but my journey is not. I will continue exploring new ways to help teams thrive in a hybrid workplace.

Thank you for reading,

—Gustavo
Chicago, March 2022

ACKNOWLEDGMENTS

Writing this book was a team effort. And while my name is on the cover, I couldn't have completed this extensive project with a wonderful group of remote, but not distant, collaborators.

My editor, Sarah Barbour, who made my ideas readable, Heather Pendley, for triple-checking the final manuscript before publication, Krishna Mohan, for the amazing cover design, and Adina Cucicov for designing the interior of the book.

The hybrid team leaders and experts who generously shared their insights and amazing stories: Tasha Eurich, Matt Mullenweg, Brian Elliott, Liz Rider, William Singleton, Darren Murph, Natasha Miller Williams, Ivan Houston, Mareike Nottrott, Jonas Wolter, Michel Bouman, Hortense le Gentil, Marissa Goldberg, Torben Friehe, Yann Leretaille,

Betsy Bula, Ozlem Brooke Erol, Myriam Hadnes, Jessica Reeder, Douglas Flory, Matt Kelly, Sarah Parsa Nguyen, Steve Urquhart, and Katya Sylvester.

The passionate gang of beta readers who reviewed the manuscript and provided invaluable feedback: Andrew O'Hearn, Letizia Migliola, Josie Iuliano, Delfino Corti, Marc McLaughlin, Silvina Cendra, Hilton Barbour, Susan Raphael, Anish Hindocha, Maren Gube, Shayne Smart, Eszter Debreczeni, Andre Braxton, Kimberley Stencel, and Patrick Van Renterghem.

All the cheerleaders who supported me along the journey—from LinkedIn pals to complete strangers who voted on the cover designs, provided feedback along the way, or put me in touch with priceless resources and people.

My wife, Moira, and my two sons, Tristan and Fausto, for their patience and letting me invade the dining table with my drafts when I got tired of being locked in my office. Most importantly, for their unconditional love and support.

BONUS PAGE

Use this QR code to access more free tools and resources.

Use this QR to access a special surprise—exclusive for readers of *Remote, Not Distant*.

NOTES

Introduction

1. Schiffer, Zoe. "Apple employees push back against returning to the office in internal letter." *The Verge*, 4 June 2021. www.theverge.com/2021/6/4/22491629/apple-employees-push-back-return-office-internal-letter-tim-cook.

2. Pope, Lauren. "I find it interesting (stupid) how WFH was considered a "vital necessity" to keep companies afloat last year." LinkedIn, accessed 28 March 2022. www.linkedin.com/posts/laurenapope_techleaders-techrecruiting-wfh-activity-6815637931013763072-Q05q.

Foundation

3. Seppälä, Emma, and Kim Cameron. "Proof That Positive Work Cultures Are More Productive." *Harvard Business Review*, December 2015. hbr.org/2015/12/proof-that-positive-work-cultures-are-more-productive.

4. Chamberlain, Andrew, and Zanele Munyikwa. "What's Culture Worth? Stock Performance of Glassdoor's Best Places to Work 2009 to 2019." *Glassdoor Economic Research*, 1 May 2021. www.glassdoor.com/research/stock-returns-bptw-2020/.

5. Silverthorne, Sean. "The Profit Power of Corporate Culture." *HBS Working Knowledge*, 28 September 2011. hbswk.hbs.edu/item/6818.html.

6. "Organizational Health Index." *McKinsey & Company*, accessed 30 March 2022. www.mckinsey.com/solutions/orgsolutions/overview/organizational-health-index.

7. Wikipedia: Sensemaking. Wikimedia Foundation, accessed 30 March 2022. en.wikipedia.org/wiki/Sensemaking.

8. Dewar, Carolyn. "Culture: 4 Keys To Why It Matters: What Separates The Highest Performing Organizations From The Rest?" *McKinsey & Company*, 28 March 2018. www.mckinsey.com/business-functions/organization/our-insights/the-organization-blog/culture-4-keys-to-why-it-matters.

9. Eaton, Kraig, et al. "The Worker-Employer Relationship Disrupted: If We Are Not A Family, What Are We?" *Deloitte Insights*, 21 July 2021. www2.deloitte.com/us/en/insights/focus/human-capital-trends.html.

Step 1: Reset Your Culture

10. Birkinshaw, Julian, et al. "Research: Knowledge Workers Are More Productive From Home." *Harvard Business Review*, 31 Aug 2021. hbr.org/2020/08/research-knowledge-workers-are-more-productive-from-home.

11. "A Community for Asynchronous Teams." accessed 30 March 2022. www.weareasync.com/.

12. Sijbrandij, Sid. Sid Sijbrandij – GitLab CEO/Cofounder. twitter.com/sytses.

13. Setty, Prasad, et al. "The Best Of Both Worlds? Making Hybrid Work." Google Workspace (webinar), accessed 30 March 2022. cloudonair.withgoogle.com/events/making-hybrid-work.

14. Fosslien, Lizz. "The Top 5 Reasons People Quit Their Jobs: It's Not Just about the Money." *Humu*, 2 November 2021. www.humu.com/blog/the-top-5-reasons-people-quit-their-jobs-its-not-just-about-the-money.

15. Stieg, Cory. "Microsoft's CEO Does This Instead Work-Life 'Balance'—and Jeff Bezos Agrees." CNBC, 24 December 2019. www.cnbc.com/2019/12/24/what-microsoft-ceo-satya-nadella-does-instead-of-work-life-balance.html.

16. Meyer, Elaine. "How to Move Your Team toward Async-First Communication." *Doist* (blog), 11 October 2021. blog.doist.com/async-first/.

17. MacLellan, Lila. "The Apple Employees' Complaint Letter is also a Road Map for Reopening Offices." *Quartz at Work*, 8 June 2021. qz.com/work/2018276/what-the-apple-employees-complaint-letter-got-right-about-hybrid/

18. "Leveling the playing field in the hybrid workplace." *Future Forum Pulse*, 25 January 2022. futureforum.com/wp-content/uploads/2022/01/Future-Forum-Pulse-Report-January-2022.pdf

19. Maurer, Roy. "Half of Workers Wish to Remain Remote Permanently." *SHRM*, 6 July 2021. www.shrm.org/hr-today/news/hr-news/pages/shrm-half-workers-wish-remain-remote-permanently.aspx.

20. Tsipursky, Gleb. "Commentary: The Psychology behind Why Some Leaders are Resisting a Hybrid Work Model." *Fortune*, 9 June 2021. fortune.com/2021/06/08/return-remote-work-hybrid-model-surveys-covid/.

21. Fried, Jason. "Hey, Marissa Mayer, You've Got It Wrong: Telecommuting Isn't a Bad Thing. It's the Future." *Inc.*, 24 October 2013. www.inc.com/jason-fried/remote-excerpt-one.html.

22. Mickos, Mårten. "It's funny we call it the virtual world." Twitter, accessed 30 March 2022. twitter.com/martenmickos.

23. Berg, Nate. "These Architects Popularized the Open Office. Now They Say 'The Open Office Is Dead.'" *Fast Company*, 19 April 2021. www.fastcompany.com/90626329/these-architects-popularized-the-open-office-now-they-say-the-open-office-is-dead.

24. Bryant, Adam. "Tobi Lütke of Shopify: Powering a Team with a 'Trust Battery.'" *The New York Times*, 24 April 2016. www.nytimes.com/2016/04/24/business/tobi-lutke-of-shopify-powering-a-team-with-a-trust-battery.html.

25. Wayland, Michael. "GM's New Remote Work Plan for Employees Is Ambiguous, Yet Surprisingly Simple: 'Work Appropriately.'" CNBC, 20 April 2021. www-cnbc-com.cdn.ampproject.org/c/s/www.cnbc.com/amp/2021/04/20/gms-simple-message-to-employees-about-return-to-work-work-appropriately.html.

26. "Best Examples of Company Cultures That Engage Employees." *Impraise* (blog), accessed 30 March 2022. blog.impraise.com/360-feedback/anarchy-or-innovation-extreme-management-policies-that-kick-it-to-the-next-level-performance-review.

27. GitLab. "The Importance of a Handbook-First Approach to Documentation." GitLab.com, accessed 30 March 2022. about.gitlab.com/company/culture/all-remote/handbook-first-documentation/.

28. Bloom, Nicholas, et al. "Does Working from Home Work?" *Stanford University*, 3 March 2015. nbloom.people.stanford.edu/sites/g/files/sbiybj4746/f/wfh.pdf.

29. Bariso, Justin. "Google Spent 2 Years Researching What Makes a Great Remote Team. It Came Up With These 3 Things." *Inc.*, accessed 30 March 2022. www.inc.com/justin-bariso/google-spent-2-years-researching-what-makes-a-great-remote-team-it-came-up-with-these-3-things.html.

30. Pinkus, Erin. "CNBC: SurveyMonkey Poll: International Women's Day 2021." SurveyMonkey.com, accessed 30 March 2022. www.surveymonkey.com/curiosity/cnbc-women-at-work-2021/.

31. Cooper, Marianne. "Research: Women Leaders Took on Even More Invisible Work during the Pandemic." *Harvard Business Review*, 13 October 2021. hbr.org/2021/10/research-women-took-on-even-more-invisible-work-during-the-pandemic.

Step 2: Reimagine a Shared Future

32. "Purpose." EY.com, accessed 30 March 2022. www.ey.com/en_gl/purpose.

33. Kenny, Graham. "Your Company's Purpose is Not its Vision, Mission, or Values." *Harvard Business Review*, 17 September 2021. hbr.org/2014/09/your-companys-purpose-is-not-its-vision-mission-or-values.

34. Polinski, Jennifer M., et al. "Impact of CVS Pharmacy's Discontinuance of Tobacco Sales on Cigarette Purchasing (2012–2014)." *American Journal of Public Health* 107, no. 4 (April 2017): 556–562. www.ncbi.nlm.nih.gov/pmc/articles/PMC5343689/#.

35. "A Message from Co-Founder and CEO Brian Chesky." *Airbnb Newsroom*, 6 May 2020. news.airbnb.com/a-message-from-co-founder-and-ceo-brian-chesky/.

36. Byars, Tessa. "Patagonia Makes Another Bold Move to Protect Public Lands." *Patagonia Works*, 22 October 2018. www.patagoniaworks.com/press/2018/10/19/patagonia-makes-another-bold-move-to-protect-public-lands.

37. Yildirmaz, Ahu. "2019 State of the Workforce Report: Full Report." *ADP Research Institute*, 2 September 2020. www.adpri.org/assets/2019-state-of-the-workforce-report/.

38. Zuzul, Tiona, et al. "Dynamic Silos: Increased Modularity in Intra-Organizational Communication Networks during the Covid-19 Pandemic." *Arxiv*, 5 September 2021. arxiv.org/pdf/2104.00641.pdf.

39. "2022 Global Talent Trends." Mercer.com, accessed 30 March 2022 www.mercer.com/our-thinking/career/global-talent-hr-trends.html.

40. Buckingham, Marcus and Ashley Goodall. "The Power of Hidden Teams." *Harvard Business Review*, 4 May 2019. https://hbr.org/2019/05/the-power-of-hidden-teams.

41. Basecamp. "What We Stand For." *Basecamp Employee Handbook*, accessed 30 March 2022. basecamp.com/handbook/02-what-we-stand-for.

42. Bariso, Justin. "Instead of Laying off 20 Percent of His Company, This CEO Made an Unusual Decision. It's a Lesson in Emotional Intelligence." *Inc.com*, 1 April 2020. www.inc.com/justin-bariso/instead-of-laying-off-20-of-his-company-this-ceo-made-an-unusual-decision-its-a-lesson-in-emotional-intelligence.html.

43. "Banker Job Cuts Will Be Back Sooner or Later." *Bloomberg*, 30 March 2020. www.bloomberg.com/opinion/articles/2020-03-30/coronavirus-banker-job-cuts-will-be-back-sooner-or-later.

44. McGregor, Jena. "The Companies That Are Pledging Not to Lay off Workers amid the Coronavirus Unemployment Crisis." *The Washington Post*, 2 April 2020. www.washingtonpost.com/business/2020/04/02/some-companies-are-pledging-not-lay-off-employees-now/.

45. Frank, Karlie. "Retailers lead mask production to combat COVID-19." National Retail Federation, 13 April 2020. nrf.com/blog/retailers-lead-mask-production-combat-covid-19.

46. "Working Towards Nearly 1 Million Masks." *Nordstrom Now*, accessed 30 March 2022. press.nordstrom.com/news-releases/news-release-details/working-towards-nearly-1-million-masks.

47. B Lab. "Looking for a B Corp? Find a B Corp: Search Here to Buy from, Work with, or Learn More about Certified B Corporations around the World." Bcorporation.net, https://www.bcorporation.net/en-us/find-a-b-corp/company/leesa-sleep

48. O'Brien, Diana, et al. "Purpose Is Everything." *Deloitte Insights*, 15 October 2019. www2.deloitte.com/us/en/insights/topics/marketing-and-sales-operations/global-marketing-trends/2020/purpose-driven-companies.html.

49. Kristof, Nicholas. "She Helped a Customer in Need. Then U.S. Bank Fired Her." *The New York Times*, 1 February 2020. www.nytimes.com/2020/02/01/opinion/sunday/us-bank-fired-employee.html.

50. Gentle, Stuart. "Half of Employees Can't Recite Their Organisation's Vision or Values." *Onrec*, 27 February 2018. www.onrec.com/news/news-archive/half-of-employees-can%E2%80%99t-recite-their-organisation%E2%80%99s-vision-or-values.

51. "Cultural Vigilance: A Corporate Imperative Insights Report." *United Minds*, accessed 30 March 2022. unitedmindsglobal.com/wp-content/uploads/2019/12/Culture-Vigilance-A-Corporate-Imperative-Insights-Report.pdf.

52. Aratani, Lori. "Boeing's New CEO Pledges Greater Transparency in Message to Employees." *The Washington Post*, 14 January 2020. www.washingtonpost.com/transportation/2020/01/14/boeings-new-ceo-pledges-greater-transparency-message-employees.

53. Lencioni, Patrick M. "Make Your Values Mean Something." *Harvard Business Review*, 1 August 2014. hbr.org/2002/07/make-your-values-mean-something.

54. Chesky, Brian. "Culture: How to Start a Startup." YouTube, accessed 30 March 2022. www.youtube.com/watch?v=RfWgVWGEuGE.

55. McKeown, Dave. "3 Pitfalls to Avoid When Building Your Core Values." *Inc.com*, 23 October 2019. www.inc.com/dave-mckeown/3-pitfalls-to-avoid-when-building-your-core-values.html.

56. Netflix. "Netflix Culture." *Netflix Jobs*, accessed 30 March 2022. https://jobs.netflix.com/culture.

57. Mike, Isaac. "Inside Uber's Aggressive, Unrestrained Workplace Culture." *New York Times*, 22 February 2017. www.nytimes.com/2017/02/22/technology/uber-workplace-culture.html.

58. Goldfein, Jocelyn. "Culture Is the Behavior You Reward and Punish." *Medium*, 1 November 2018. jocelyngoldfein.com/culture-is-the-behavior-you-reward-and-punish-7e8e75c6543e.

59. Sull, Donald, and Stefano Turconi. "When It Comes to Culture, Does Your Company Walk the Talk?" *MIT Sloan Management Review*, 21 July 2020. sloanreview.mit.edu/article/when-it-comes-to-culture-does-your-company-walk-the-talk/.

60. Carnes, Molly, et al. "Promises and Pitfalls of Diversity Statements: Proceed With Caution." *Academic Medicine : Journal of the Association of American Medical Colleges* 94, no. 1 (2019):20-24. doi:10.1097/ACM.0000000000002388.

61. Hindocha, Anish. Anish Hindocha – ITV Change Lead. LinkedIn. uk.linkedin.com/in/anishhindocha.

62. Shear, Emmett. "Your Culture Is Determined by What People Perceive to Be the Behaviors You Reward and Punish." Twitter, 9 June 2021. twitter.com/eshear/status/1402449679363633155?s=20.

63. Foer, Franklin. "Jeff Bezos's Master Plan." *The Atlantic*, November 2019. https://www.theatlantic.com/magazine/archive/2019/11/what-jeff-bezos-wants/598363.

64. Isaacson, Walter. *Steve Jobs: The Exclusive Biography.* New York: Simon & Schuster, 2021. www.amazon.com/Steve-Jobs-Walter-Isaacson/dp/1451648537.

Step 3: Reignite Belonging

65. Johnson, Whitney, et al. "The Value of Belonging at Work." *Harvard Business Review*, 21 December 2021. hbr.org/2019/12/the-value-of-belonging-at-work.

66. Walters, Shona. "Here's How to Build a Sense of Belonging in the Workplace." *Better Up* (blog), 11 May 2021. www.betterup.com/blog/belonging#:~:text=BetterUp%20research%20shows%20that%20fostering,impact%20on%20a%20company's%20revenue.

67. Edmondson, Amy C. Faculty & Research – Harvard Business School. www.hbs.edu/faculty/Pages/profile.aspx?facId=6451.

68. Herway, Jake. "How to Create a Culture of Psychological Safety." Gallup.com, 4 January 2022. www.gallup.com/workplace/236198/create-culture-psychological-safety.aspx.

69. "Re:Work." Google.com, accessed 30 March 2022. rework.withgoogle.com/print/guides/5721312655835136/.

70. Kosner, Anthony Wing. "Amy Edmondson on the Power of Psychological Safety in Distributed Work." Dropbox: Work in Progress, 27 March 2021.

blog.dropbox.com/topics/work-culture/amy-edmondson-on-the-power-of-psychological-safety-in-distribute.

71. Kohn, Nicholas W., and Steven M. Smith. "Collaborative Fixation: Effects of Others' Ideas on Brainstorming." *Applied Cognitive Psychology* 25, no. 3 (2010):359–371. doi.org/10.1002/acp.1699

72. Hsieh, Tony. "Culture Book." *Zappos Insights*, accessed 30 March 2022. www.zapposinsights.com/culture-book.

73. Gino, Francesca. "How Women Can Learn from Even Biased Feedback." *HBS Working Knowledge*, 1 September 2021. hbswk.hbs.edu/item/how-women-can-learn-from-even-biased-feedback.

74. Schwartz, Jeffrey, et al. "Changing the Conversations That Kill Your Culture." *Strategy+Business*, 26 April 2018. www.strategy-business.com/article/Changing-the-Conversations-That-Kill-Your-Culture.

75. Cleanaway. "About Us" (media releases), 20 January 2021. www.cleanaway.com.au/about-us/media-releases/.

76. Buckingham, Marcus, and Ashley Goodall. "Why Feedback Rarely Does What It's Meant To." *Harvard Business Review*, 4 February 2022. hbr.org/2019/03/the-feedback-fallacy.

77. Werber, Cassie. "New Evidence Suggests Women Get Kinder, Less Honest Feedback at Work." *Quartz*, 30 June 2021. qz.com/work/1859145/women-get-kinder-less-honest-feedback-at-work/.

78. Staley, Oliver. "A Kinder, Gentler Microsoft is Replacing Feedback with 'Perspectives." *Quartz at Work*, 10 September 2018. qz.com/work/1380162/a-kinder-gentler-microsoft-is-replacing-feedback-with-perspectives.

79. Di Fiore, Alessandro, and Marco Souza. "Are Peer Reviews the Future of Performance Evaluations?" *Harvard Business Review*, 12 January 2021. hbr.org/2021/01/are-peer-reviews-the-future-of-performance-evaluations.

80. Wiles, Jackie. "Peer Feedback Boosts Employee Performance." *Gartner*, 11 May 2018. www.gartner.com/smarterwithgartner/peer-feedback-boosts-employee-performance/.

81. Fitzii. "Harness the Power of an Entire Talent Acquisition Team with One Smart Tool." Fitzii.com, accessed 30 March 2022. www.fitzii.com/.

82. Sellgren, Johan. Johan Sellgren – Spotify Global HR Business Partner. LinkedIn, accessed 30 March 2022. se.linkedin.com/in/johan-sellgren-he-him-9274896.

83. Huston, Therese. "Giving Critical Feedback Is Even Harder Remotely." *Harvard Business Review*, 26 January 2021. hbr.org/2021/01/giving-critical-feedback-is-even-harder-remotely.

84. Wikipedia: Fundamental Attribution Error. Wikimedia Foundation, 10 February 2022. en.wikipedia.org/wiki/Fundamental_attribution_error.

85. Horowitz, Ben. "Ben Horowitz's Best Startup Advice." *Medium*, Product Hunt, 28 March 2018. https://blog.producthunt.com/ben-horowitz-s-best-startup-advice-7e8c09c8de1b

86. The Eurich Group. "Dr. Tasha Eurich: The Eurich Group." www.tashaeurich.com/.

87. Bischof, Jackie. "How Do You Resolve Conflict in the Hybrid Workplace?" *Quartz*, 16 November 2021. qz.com/work/2089523/how-do-you-resolve-conflict-in-the-hybrid-workplace/.

88. Hinds, Pamela J., and Mark Mortensen. "Understanding Conflict in Geographically Distributed Teams." *Organization Science* 16, no. 3 (May–June 2005):290-307. doi.org/10.1287/orsc.1050.0122.

89. Peham, Thomas. "The benefits of asynchronous design feedback." Usersnap (blog), accessed March 30, 2022. usersnap.com/blog/asynchronous-design-feedback.

90. Thomas, Owen. "Etsy's winning secret: don't play the blame game!" *Insider*, 15 May 2012. www.businessinsider.com/etsy-chad-dickerson-blameless-post-mortem-2012-5.

91. World Rugby. "Latest All Blacks Haka intimidates the French." YouTube, 17 October 2015. www.youtube.com/watch?v=PptTeyYShdw.

92. Savina, Anna. "Suneet Bhatt on the best onboarding practices for a distributed startup." *Miro*, accessed March 30, 2022. miro.com/blog/suneet-bhatt-employee-onboarding-distributed-team.

Step 4: Rethink Collaboration

93. Mullen, Brian, et al. "Productivity Loss in Brainstorming Groups: A Meta-Analytic Integration." Taylor & Francis Online. 7 Jun 2010. www.tandfonline.com/doi/abs/10.1207/s15324834basp1201_1.

94. Hansen, Morten T. "When Internal Collaboration Is Bad for Your Company." *Harvard Business Review*, April 2009. hbr.org/2009/04/when-internal-collaboration-is-bad-for-your-company.

95. Cross, Rob, et al. "Collaboration Without Burnout." *Harvard Business Review*, July-August 2008. hbr.org/2018/07/collaboration-without-burnout.

96. Osborne, Hilary. "Home workers putting in more hours since Covid, research shows." *The Guardian*, 4 February 2021. www.theguardian.com/business/2021/feb/04/home-workers-putting-in-more-hours-since-covid-research.

97. Carmichael, Sarah Green. "The Research Is Clear: Long Hours Backfire for People and for Companies." Harvard Business Review, 19 August

2015. hbr.org/2015/08/the-research-is-clear-long-hours-backfire-for-people-and-for-companies.

98. Derks, Daantje, et al. "Smartphone use and work–home interference: The moderating role of social norms and employee work." *Journal of Occupational and Organizational Psychology* 88 (2015):155–177. engagementwww.isonderhouden.nl/doc/pdf/arnoldbakker/articles/articles_arnold_bakker_379.pdf.

99. Hackston, John, and Nikita Dhost. "Type and email communication." OPP, 2016. eu.themyersbriggs.com/-/media/2c27b0950f1f478da89de20362258e0d.ashx.

100. Quinones, C., et al. "Compulsive Internet use and workaholism: An exploratory two-wave longitudinal study." *Computers in Human Behavior* 60 (2016):492-499, www.academia.edu/23202544/Quinones_C._Griffiths_M.D._and_Kakabadse_N._2016_._Compulsive_Internet_use_and_workaholism_An_exploratory_two-wave_longitudinal_study._Computers_in_Human_Behavior_60_492-499.

101. Future Forum. "Leveling the playing field in the hybrid workplace," *Future Forum Pulse*, January 2022. Futureforum.com/wp-content/uploads/2022/01/Future-Forum-Pulse-Report-January-2022.pdf.

102. Baker, Mary. "4 Modes of Collaboration Are Key to Success in Hybrid Work," *Gartner*, 14 June 2021. www.gartner.com/smarterwithgartner/4-modes-of-collaboration-are-key-to-success-in-hybrid-work.

103. "The Origins of Herman Miller's Modes of Work," *HermanMiller Living Office*, 2013. static1.squarespace.com/static/5a332791914e6bb12028c8b8/t/5a37f5eb0d92972a19b25bf8/1513616885923/The+Origins+of+Herman+Miller%27s+Modes+of+Work.pdf.

104. Gensler Research Institute. *Gensler Research & Insight*, accessed March 30, 2022. www.gensler.com/gri.

105. Newport, Cal. *Deep Work: Rules for Focused Success in a Distracted World, 1st edition.* New York: Grand Central Publishing, 2016.

106. "Anatomy of Work Index 2021: Overcoming Disruption in a Distributed World." Asana.com, 2021. resources.asana.com/rs/784-XZD-582/images/PDF-FY21-Global-EN-Anatomy of Work Report.pdf.

107. Garn, Randy. "5 Benefits of a Design Sprint," LinkedIn, 3 April 2020. www.linkedin.com/pulse/5-benefits-design-sprint-randy-garn.

108. Miller, Claire Cain. "Do Chance Meetings at the Office Boost Innovation? There's No Evidence of It." *The New York Times*, 23 June 2021. nytimes.com/2021/06/23/upshot/remote-work-innovation-office.html.

109. Lavinia, Sahil. "Going fully remote was nice, but the real benefit was in going fully asynchronous." Twitter, 29 January 2020, 7:41 a.m. twitter.com/shl/status/1222545212477599751.

110. Sutton, Bob. "Why Big Teams Suck: Seven (Plus or Minus Two) Is the Magical Number Once Again." Work Matters, 3 March 2014. bobsutton. typepad.com/my_weblog/2014/03/why-big-teams-suck-seven-plus-or-minus-two-is-the-magical-number-once-again.html.

111. "The Most Powerful Time Management Technique You're Probably Not Using." *Nir and Far*, accessed March 30, 2022. www.nirandfar.com/timeboxing.

112. "GitLab OnBoarding Buddies." *GitLab Handbook* accessed March 30, 2022. about.gitlab.com/handbook/people-group/general-onboarding/onboarding-buddies.

113. "How and Why to Create an Onboarding Buddy Program." *Zavvy*, 11 March 2022. www.zavvy.io/blog/onboarding-buddy-program.

114. Burkus, David. "Make Your Remote Team "Feel" Like a Team." *Harvard Business Review*, 11 February 2021. hbr.org/2021/02/make-your-remote-team-feel-like-a-team.

115. Miller, Lucas. "How Slack ruined work." *Wired*, 13 January 2020. www.wired.co.uk/article/slack-ruining-work.

116. Newport, Cal. "Slack Is the Right Tool for the Wrong Way to Work." *The New Yorker*, 14 December 2020. www.newyorker.com/culture/cultural-comment/slack-is-the-right-tool-for-the-wrong-way-to-work.

Step 5: Release Agility

117. Beckstrand, Gary. "Employee engagement is out. Here's a better metric." *Fast Company*, 8 February 2022. www.fastcompany.com/90719359/employee-engagement-is-out-heres-a-better-metric.

118. "Leveling the playing field in the hybrid workplace." *Future Forum Pulse*, January 2022. Futureforum.com/wp-content/uploads/2022/01/Future-Forum-Pulse-Report-January-2022.pdf.

119. "Future Forum Study Reveals That Hybrid Has Become the Dominant Work Model for Global Knowledge Workers." *Business Wire*, 25 January 2022. www.businesswire.com/news/home/20220125005572/en/Future-Forum-Study-Reveals-That-Hybrid-Has-Become-the-Dominant-Work-Model-for-Global-Knowledge-Workers-Ensuring-Equity-Between-Remote-and-In-Office-Employees-Moves-to-the-Top-of-Executives%E2%80%99-Priority.

120. Fraser, Jane. "Latest Update on the Future of Work at Citi." *Citigroup*, 24 March 2021. blog.citigroup.com/2021/03/latest-update-on-the-future-of-work-at-citi.

121. Burke, Katie. "The Future of Work at HubSpot: How We're Building a Hybrid Company." HubSpot, updated 25 September 2020. https://www.hubspot.com/careers-blog/future-of-work-hybrid.

122. Somers, Meredith. "Dropbox CEO: 3 insights from leading a 'virtual first' workforce." *MIT Management Sloan School*, 27 October 21. mitsloan.mit. edu/ideas-made-to-matter/dropbox-ceo-3-insights-leading-a-virtual-first-workforce.

123. Mullenweg, Matt. "Distributed Work's Five Levels of Autonomy." *Matt Mullenweg Unlucky in Cards*, 10 April 2020. ma.tt/2020/04/ five-levels-of-autonomy.

124. "Culture Code: Creating A Lovable Company." *HubSpot*, 20 March 2013. www.slideshare.net/HubSpot/the-hubspot-culture-code-creating-a-company-we-love.

125. Hastings, Reed. *No Rules Rules: Netflix and the Culture of Reinvention*. New York: Penguin Press, 2020.

126. Wikipedia: Theory X and Theory Y. Wikimedia Foundation, 3 February 2022. en.wikipedia.org/wiki/Theory_X_and_Theory_Y.

127. Laloux, Frederic. "Safe Space." *Reinventing Organizations Wiki,* accessed March 30, 2022. reinventingorganizationswiki.com/theory/safe-space.

128. "The Best Companies for Remote Workers 2021." *Quartz*, accessed March 30, 2022. qz.com/se/best-companies-for-remote-workers-2021.

129. Gross, Jenny. "The Limits of Vacation." *The New York Times*, 14 August 2021. www.nytimes.com/2021/08/14/business/dealbook/vacation-burnout.html.

130. "Distributed-First Is the Future of Work at Spotify." *Spotify: For the Record*, 12 February 2021. newsroom.spotify.com/2021-02-12/ distributed-first-is-the-future-of-work-at-spotify.

131. "The Next Great Disruption Is Hybrid Work—Are We Ready?" Microsoft, 22 March 2021. www.microsoft.com/en-us/worklab/work-trend-index/ hybrid-work.

132. "The importance of a handbook-first approach to documentation." *GitLab Handbook*, accessed March 30, 2022. about.gitlab.com/company/culture/ all-remote/handbook-first-documentation.

133. "How We Hire Developers." *Automattic*, accessed March 30, 2022. automattic.com/work-with-us/how-we-hire-developers.

134. MacKay, Jory. "Managing interruptions at work: What we learned surveying hundreds of RescueTime users about their worst distractions." *RescueTime*, 29 May 2018, blog.rescuetime.com/interruptions-at-work.

135. Lovallo, Dan, and Olivier Sibony. "The case for behavioral strategy." *McKinsey*, 1 March 2010. www.mckinsey.com/business-functions/ strategy-and-corporate-finance/our-insights/the-case-for-behavioral-strategy.

136. Bezos, Jeff. "2016 Letter to Shareholders." *About Amazon*, 17 April 2017. www.aboutamazon.com/news/company-news/2016-letter-to-shareholders.

137. McElheran, Kristina, and Erik Brynjolfsson. "The Rise of Data-Driven Decision Making Is Real but Uneven." *Harvard Business Review*, 3 February 2016. hbr.org/2016/02/the-rise-of-data-driven-decision-making-is-real-but-uneven.

138. Lenzen, Manuela. "Feeling Our Emotions." *Scientific American,* 1 April 2005. www.scientificamerican.com/article/feeling-our-emotions.

139. Lashinsky, Adam. "How Apple Works: Inside the World's Biggest Startup." *Fortune*, 25 August 2011. fortune.com/2011/08/25/how-apple-works-inside-the-worlds-biggest-startup.

140. Greenfield, Rebecca. "Airbnb Apologizes to the Woman with a Ransacked Apartment." *The Atlantic*, 1 August 2011. www.theatlantic.com/technology/archive/2011/08/airbnb-apologizes-woman-ransacked-apartment/353549.

141. Duke, Annie. *How to Decide: Simple Tools for Making Better Choices.* Portfolio/Penguin, 2020.

142. Le Gentil, Hortense. "Leaders, Stop Trying to Be Heroes." *Harvard Business Review*, 25 October 2021. hbr.org/2021/10/leaders-stop-trying-to-be-heroes.

143. Cohen, Arianne. "The surprising traits of good remote leaders." BBC, 9 September 2021. www.bbc.com/worklife/article/20200827-why-in-person-leaders-may-not-be-the-best-virtual-ones.

Afterword

144. Entis, Laura. "Google calls workers back to offices." LinkedIn, accessed 30 March 2022. www.linkedin.com/news/story/google-calls-workers-back-to-offices-5742442.

Made in the USA
Monee, IL
02 January 2023

20363583R00184